THE SPECTRE OF PHILIP

SOURCES IN ANCIENT HISTORY

General Editor: E. A. Judge, Macquarie University

This series is designed to provide translations of substantial bodies of source material with accompanying discussion particularly suitable for tutorial use by students of ancient history or of political and social institutions.

THE SPECTRE OF PHILIP
J. R. Ellis and R. D. Milns

THE ATHENIAN HALF-CENTURY
A. French

THE SPECTRE OF PHILIP

Demosthenes' First *Philippic*, *Olynthiacs* and Speech *On the Peace*

A STUDY IN HISTORICAL EVIDENCE

J. R. Ellis and R. D. Milns

SYDNEY UNIVERSITY PRESS

SYDNEY UNIVERSITY PRESS
Press Building, University of Sydney

Great Britain, Europe, North America
INTERNATIONAL SCHOLARLY BOOK SERVICES, INC.

First published 1970
© J. R. Ellis and R. D. Milns 1970
Library of Congress Catalog Card Number 76-135112
National Library of Australia registry card number and
ISBN 0 424 06120 1

This book is supported by money from
THE ELEANOR SOPHIA WOOD BEQUEST

Printed in Australia at The Griffin Press, Adelaide
and registered in Australia for transmission by post as a book

CONTENTS

Preface	vii
Translator's Preface	x
Abbreviations	xi
General Introduction	1
Libanius' Introduction to the Speeches of Demosthenes	7

PHILIPPIC I (Speech IV)

Preface to Speech IV	11
Libanius' Introduction to Speech IV	15
Translation and Commentary: *Philippic* I —c.January 350(?)	16

THE *OLYNTHIACS* (Speeches II, I, and III)

Preface to the *Olynthiacs*	34
Libanius' Introduction to Speech I	39
Libanius' Introduction to Speech II	42
Libanius' Introduction to Speech III	43
Translation and Commentary: *Olynthiac* II —August/September(?) 349	44
Translation and Commentary: *Olynthiac* I —August/September(?) 349	55
Translation and Commentary: *Olynthiac* III —c.September(?) 349	65

Contents

ON THE PEACE (Speech V)

    Preface to Speech V   77

    Libanius' Introduction to Speech V   81

    Translation and Commentary: *On the Peace* —late 346   83

Appendixes

    The Theorikon   91

    Selection of Historical Fragments   94

    Selection of Relevant Inscriptions   102

    The Attic Year   108

    Chronological Table — Summer 352 BC to late autumn 346 BC   109

    Table of Extant Genuine Speeches of Demosthenes to 341   113

Select Bibliography   115

Index   120

PREFACE

With a choice from the Demosthenic corpus of sixty-odd speeches of which over thirty appear to be genuine, or, more importantly, of sixteen public speeches of which probably twelve were written and spoken by Demosthenes, the first difficulty in planning this book, limited as it must be in size, was the choice of material. This was further compounded by the fact that many important points of historical evidence are derived from the orator's private speeches and, especially, from the two major works, *On the False Embassy* and *On the Crown*.

We had, then, to make a fairly narrow choice in the midst of plenty. Where we might have wished a selection that would serve to illustrate the progress of Demosthenes' career, or of Philip's, we were prevented by the sheer bulk of the necessary material.

With the restriction of size governed by the purpose of this book, we were forced to look for a smaller theme—smaller, that is, in the volume of evidence available. We have not chosen the five speeches translated here because they provide us with a picture of Demosthenes' career; 5 years, the period they cover, is a short time. Nor, for the same reason, have we chosen them to illustrate Philip's progress. The problem was what aspects of the whole subject we might hope to cover with any pretence to fulness.

These five speeches were delivered at a time when Athens was becoming properly aware for the first time of the power and potential threat of Macedon. They are the public voice—or as much as we can know of it—of the man who led the adverse reaction of many Athenians to Philip. Demosthenes' chief opponent in his earlier career, Eubulus, to whose policies the former had adhered until not long before 350 BC, maintained the leading influence over the Athenian people from about 355 until after 346. By 343, when the first great test of strength between the rival policies took place, Demosthenes was perhaps the most influential man in Athens, at least where foreign policy was concerned; he narrowly failed in that year to convict Aeschines, the supporter of Eubulus, of misconduct in the second embassy to Macedon of 346, in spite of the extreme weakness of his case. These five speeches are the extant means whereby our orator developed from the follower of Eubulus to the point where, given the disillusionment of many Athenians after the peace between Philip and Athens in 346, he was the obvious man for the people to follow.

What we have attempted to provide, then, is a study in political manoeuvre and in historical evidence—with this proviso, that our aim, rather than to try to answer all the problems, has been to collect for the reader the relevant source-material and to indicate where to look for help in its interpretation. This is a book that, because of its limited size and purpose, is intended for use in conjunction with the standard works of the period.

It has been inevitable that later interpretations of Philip have been influenced very strongly by the judgements of Demosthenes; he provides the great bulk of the extant information on the Macedonian king. But beyond this, it has been the case for several centuries that the student in the English and the European classical tradition has almost always approached Demosthenes first of all as the greatest exponent of Greek oratory and only subsequently as a source for Philip. Hence the unhappy situation in which Philip has been seen by almost every scholar predominantly through the eyes of one of his greatest enemies—in much the same way as peoples like the Phoenicians, Philistines, Edomites, and so on, are known to us largely or entirely through the writings of their enemies, the Jews, or as England's Richard III has suffered, at least until recently, from the bias of the Tudor historians.

To carry this point a little further, it is useful to compare relatively modern studies of Alexander the Great with those of Philip. There is tremendous disparity, to be sure, in the relative volume of evidence bearing on these two men, but the great difference is that Alexander's career was recorded in the main by those who admired him (see, for example, Arr. I.12, for a far from contemporary view but one that underscores the leanings of a writer who more than any other has influenced modern scholarship on Alexander). In the cases of Richard III and Alexander the Great, recent scholarship has tended to reinterpret the evidence so as to revise, often drastically, the traditional viewpoint, but Philip has as yet inspired no such movement. This is not to say that every study has been coloured by Demosthenes' hatred for Philip—far from it. Several influential German historians of the late nineteenth century, for example, saw in Demosthenes a reactionary fighting a hopeless battle against a great unification movement, led by Philip, inevitably superseding the particularism of the *polis* organization. But here again, though more subtly, Philip is seen from the Athenian, or rather Greek standpoint, though because there is no sympathy with the opposition he inspired he becomes the hero instead of the villain. There has been no genuine attempt to see Philip as the Macedonian king and only incidentally as the Athenian arch-enemy.

Preface

The prerequisite for any such attempt is a careful examination of what evidence we have, especially the evidence of Demosthenes, as being the most detailed to survive. It is to this end that we have selected the five speeches of this book, on the understanding that a study of Demosthenes' motives in furthering his own career and in opposing Philip is a step in this direction. It is an introduction to the evaluation of Demosthenes' worth as a source for Philip.

As well as the speeches, Professor Milns has translated the relevant Introductions of Libanius, a much later commentator on the orator. We include these for two reasons: first, that they provide us with one man's interpretation of the speeches—however unsophisticated and uncritical we may sometimes find it—and, second, that as far as we know there is no other accessible English translation of them. They serve in some measure as a condensation and interpretation of the speeches and also as an example of the treatment of literary evidence—even if an example few now would be likely to find acceptable.

I have not always tried to give full references to modern works, nor, for events not directly connected with the speeches and their period, to all relevant ancient works; in these cases I have given only enough guidance for the reader who is particularly interested in such points in the search for further evidence. The main standard works on Demosthenes and Philip and their period (for which reviews are cited in the Bibliography) treat all or most of the points raised in this book and are cited normally only in cases of particular emphasis or when the evidence seems to contradict their conclusions. Further, where a recent work refers to earlier treatments of the problem or problems with which it is concerned or from which it follows, I have been content to cite only the later work. The stress, partly from considerations of space, partly from the lack of need for most students to pursue the argument itself to its modern origins, is always on where to start looking.

Finally, we were both conscious—we could hardly be otherwise—of inconsistencies in the English rendering of Greek proper names. In general, where a name is normally known in its Latinized or Anglicized form (as, for example: 'Byzantium' for 'Byzantion', 'Potidaea' for 'Poteidaia', 'Philip' for 'Philippos', etc.) we have adhered to the convention. But usually when a name is less generally known we have simply transliterated the Greek (as, for example: 'Heraion Teichos', 'Koroneia', etc.), as with technical terms (*hipparchos, trierarchia,* etc.).

We wish to express our gratitude to Mr G. R. Stanton, of the University of New England, for help in preparing early drafts and to Professor E. A. Judge, of Macquarie University, for advice and help at all stages.

Monash University   J.R.E.

TRANSLATOR'S PREFACE

The text followed throughout (with one exception) is *Orationes* edited by S. H. Butcher and W. Rennie in the Oxford Classical Text series (Oxford University Press, London 1903-1931). Of English translations of Demosthenes' speeches I have occasionally consulted those of T. Leland, *Orations of Demosthenes* (London 1825); C. R. Kennedy, *The Olynthiac and Other Public Orations of Demosthenes* (London 1889); J. H. Vince, *Demosthenes*, Vol. I (Loeb Classical Library, Heinemann, London 1954); and A. W. Pickard-Cambridge, *Public Orations* (Demosthenes) (Everyman's Library, Dent, London 1906; reprinted 1963). The responsibility for the translation offered, however, lies entirely with myself. Of critical editions of the speeches I have found that of the *Olynthiac Speeches* edited by J. M. Macgregor (Pitt Press, Cambridge 1950) most useful in the interpretation of some grammatical points.

The general principle of translation adopted is based on the fact that this book is intended for the use of students of ancient history who have no knowledge of Greek but who want to know as exactly as possible what Demosthenes said. I have therefore kept the translation as close to the original Greek as is consistent with English usage, even though this may result at times in a certain inelegance of expression. For any mistakes in the translation the responsibility is entirely mine.

University of Queensland   R.D.M.

ABBREVIATIONS

Commonly cited works are referred to by the author's surname; these are asterisked in the Bibliography where details may be found.

Aes.	Aeschines I (*Against Timarchus*)
	II (*On the Embassy*)
	III (*Against Ctesiphon*)
AJA	American Journal of Archaeology
AJPh	American Journal of Philology
Andoc.	Andocides I (*On the Mysteries*)
Androtion	Androtion, *Atthis*, fragments
Ar.	Aristophanes, *The Birds*
	The Clouds
Arist.	Aristotle, *Athenian Constitution* (or *Ath. Pol.*)
	Economics
	Nicomachian Ethics
Aristid.	Aelius Aristides, *Panathenaecus*
Arr.	Arrian, *Anabasis of Alexander*
Athenaeus	Athenaeus, *The Deipnosophists*
BCH	*Bulletin de Correspondance Hellénique*
CAH	*Cambridge Ancient History*
C&M	*Classica et Mediaevalia*
CJ	*Classical Journal*
CPh	*Classical Philology*
CQ	*Classical Quarterly*
CR	*Classical Review*
*Ddf.	G. Dindorf *see* Bibliography
Dem. (D. in notes)	Demosthenes
D. Hal.	Dionysius of Halicarnassus, *Letters to Ammaeus*
Dinarchus	Dinarchus I (*Against Demosthenes*)
DS	Diodorus Siculus, *Library of History*
Front.	Frontinus, *Stratagems*
G&R	*Greece and Rome*
Hdt.	Herodotus, *Histories*
IG	*Inscriptiones Graecae*
Isaeus	Isaeus VIII (*On the Estate of Ciron*)

Abbreviations

Isoc.	Isocrates XV (*Antidosis*)
	VI (*Archidamus*)
	VII (*Areopagiticus*)
	VIII (*On the Peace*)
	V (*Philippus*)
	XIV (*Plataecus*)
JHS	*Journal of Hellenic Studies*
Just.	Justin, *Historiae Philippicae*
Lys.	Lysias, XX (*For Polystratus*)
	XXI (*Defence against a Charge of Bribery*)
Nepos	Cornelius Nepos, *Life of Aristides*
	Life of Chabrias
	Life of Iphicrates
	Life of Timotheus
NumChron	*Numismatic Chronicle*
OCD	*The Oxford Classical Dictionary*
Paus.	Pausanias, *Description of Greece*
PCPhS	*Proceedings of the Cambridge Philological Society*
Philochorus	Philochorus, *Atthis*, fragments
Plato	Plato, *Meno*
	Phaedo
	Phaedrus
Plut.	Plutarch, *Life of Alexander*
	Life of Aristides
	Life of Demosthenes
	Life of Nicias
	Life of Pericles
	Life of Phocion
	Life of Theseus
	Moralia
Poll.	Pollux, *Onomastikon*
Polyaenus	Polyaenus, *Stratagems*
Ps-Xen.	Pseudo-Xenophon, *Athenian Constitution* ('The Old Oligarch')
RE	*Real-encyclopaedie der classischen Altertumswissenschaft*
REA	*Revue des Études Anciennes*
REG	*Revue des Études Grecques*
RIDA	*Revue Internationale des Droits de l'Antiquité*
RhM	*Rheinisches Museum für Philologie*
Strabo	Strabo, *Geography*
Suet.	Suetonius, *Life of Caligula*

Abbreviations

Theopompus	Theopompus, *Philippica*, fragments
Thuc.	Thucydides, *Histories*
WS	*Wiener Studien*
Xen.	Xenophon, *Anabasis*
	Hellenica (HG: *Historia Graeca*)

GENERAL INTRODUCTION

The sources for any study of Demosthenes and Philip are very poor. Very often, even on matters of the order and dating of events, the evidence is simply too scant for definite judgement. But the problem is even more pronounced when we look for evaluations of the reasons for Philip's actions; for although no historian can accept uncritically the self-justification of any man for his own policy such material if it survives does serve to remind him that such a point of view exists. And Philip's interpretation of his own actions is almost unknown to us.[1]

Only five contemporary authors have left us much of value on the period 359 to 336 BC. The works of two of these, the historians Ephorus and Theopompus, have been for the most part lost. The fragments that remain are of limited value—in the case of Ephorus because where he might have been most helpful he does not survive,[2] and in the case of Theopompus because for the greater part he has survived through lexicographers and the like, who were concerned mainly with the names and spelling of out-of-the-way places, and through Athenaeus, whose interest was primarily in unusual stories—the more sensational the better —of the ilk suitable for retailing at the dinner-table. Of the useful extant fragments relatively few help to illuminate the Macedonian situation.[3] We are left then with three Athenian political figures, Isocrates, Aeschines, and Demosthenes.

Isocrates, a political philosopher and teacher of the arts of oratory and history, sheds more light, when he writes to Philip, on himself than on the Macedonian king. He preserves for us far less of what Philip thought

[1] Cf. Dem. XII ('Philip's Letter'), purporting to be Philip's statement of his position in 340. It may be spurious but, if so, is believed to have been written by a tutor of Alexander, the historian Anaximenes of Lampsacus, whom we may expect to have known enough of Philip's intentions to make this a useful document. Cf. also Dem. XVIII.77-78, again probably a forgery but useful.

[2] Diodorus uses him in Book XVI as a source for Philip down to 357/6, but only occasionally thereafter; cf. Hammond, CQ 1937, 77-91, esp. 85-9, and CQ 1938, 148-51. Where Diodorus was not able to use Ephorus he seems to have relied for his information on Philip on Diyllus, an Athenian historian whose anti-Macedonian viewpoint is clear.

[3] The fragments of Anaximenes' *Hellenica* and *Philippica* are helpful but very few in number; some fragments of the *Atthis* of Philochorus survive. Cf. our Appendix, 'Selection of Historical Fragments'.

The Spectre of Philip

and did than of what he considered Philip ought to think and do. His value is therefore limited, the more so because whatever his own worth he does not seem to have represented any important stream of Athenian or Greek thought.[4]

Aeschines, one of the chief opponents of Demosthenes and supporter of Eubulus, has left us three speeches, two of which are concerned in part with Philip. But for all this orator's opposition to Demosthenes and for all Demosthenes' charges of treachery he is first and foremost an Athenian and, moreover, an Athenian politician; he speaks well of Philip when he perceives him to be acting for the benefit of Athens (or Aeschines), but has little or no understanding of, or sympathy for, Macedonian interests. That is, although he may serve often as a corrective to Demosthenes on some points, we may not expect—nor do we find —anything remotely approaching the value of a Macedonian source in his speeches.

Eleven of Demosthenes' extant speeches are devoted largely to Philip, or, more specifically, to attacks against him.[5] It will not surprise us then to find that the modern picture of the Macedonian king has been determined largely by the judgement of the Athenian orator, the author of so great a bulk of the evidence, the man who was also his greatest single enemy. This anti-Macedonian weight of the evidence has led to the modern acceptance often of even the most unbalanced criticisms. The oft-repeated claim of Demosthenes[6]—that Philip was a local despot whose lust for power allowed him no rest while territory remained unconquered —was probably believed by many Athenians, especially after the fall of Olynthus,[7] and this is perhaps understandable from that point of view. But while we may concede this, we have also to evaluate Philip's career from the Macedonian viewpoint; he was the king of Macedonia and his responsibility was to the interests of his country, not to the satisfaction of Athens. As Cawkwell[8] has pointed out, further, 'the key to the understanding of the relations of Greece and Macedon is to be found not in the realms of morals and moral decline but in strategy and military power'. The rise of a strong national state, with its national standing army, altered the balance of power around the Aegean. This was a fact, a fact perhaps that once-successful city-states excusably could not foresee and resisted for all they were worth but one that had nothing to do with morals.

However, we are nevertheless entitled to ask the reason for the expan-

[4] Cf. Perlman, *Historia* 1957, 306-17, for an evaluation of Isocrates' proposals to Philip.
[5] Nos IV, II, I, III, V, VI, XIX, VIII, IX, X, XVIII, in chronological order.
[6] For example, II.6-10, I.13-15, III.8-9, etc.
[7] Cf. Preface to Speech V.
[8] *JHS* 1963, 67.

sion of this national state, and Demosthenes still provides our only contemporary evaluation. But while making use of him, our task is to assess this reason from the Macedonian point of view.

The purpose of this book is not to attempt to provide an answer. But three questions may at least point the way by which answers may be arrived at. Firstly, is it possible to explain what Philip did as necessary to safeguard the Macedonian interest? If it can be said (given the strategically important position of Macedonia in the northern Aegean and given its proximity to the rich mines of Mount Pangaeus in western Thrace and to the timber resources of the area, all of which had given other states, especially Athens, such an interest in keeping Macedonia weak) that the loss of initiative by a Macedonia for the first time gaining a real national identity was the passing of that initiative to her enemies, then by any standard a Macedonian king with the power to do so must seize it. Specifically, if Macedonia would be endangered by Philip's failure to resort to intrigue and force to close his borders, to safeguard his throne, and to keep at bay his powerful neighbour the Chalcidian League and his more distant but more powerful enemy Athens, then by adopting these methods where necessary Philip, by the most relevant standard, would be discharging his royal duty—certainly, at least, by the standards of his day.

Secondly, was Philip hated and feared by all good Greeks? This impression is given by Demosthenes and he is quick to label dissenters as traitors[9]—but not all Greeks shared this opinion. To some, especially to those who had long suffered under the yoke of Spartan hegemony, Philip came as a deliverer.[10] One yoke for another, says Demosthenes.[11] The most effective rebuttal comes from Polybius:[12] these men and cities named by Demosthenes were fully justified in acting in their own interests; it was their duty not to fight against Philip but to take every step for their own honour and glory. They were not traitors to the Greek cause—if such a thing could be said to have existed. The cause for which Demosthenes fought was *Athenian*, and the smaller states had suffered for centuries under such causes. Was Demosthenes right, that they were exchanging one master for another? They did not think so, and, if we may accept Polybius' word, in the long as well as the short term they were convinced that their decision was the correct one. Demosthenes implicitly concedes that there was something in their point of view, but that it was a better thing to suffer at the hands of true brothers, like the Athenians or the Spartans, than to submit to a 'pestilent

[9] For example, IX.34-52, 56-67.
[10] Cf. Pausanias IV.27.10, VI.11.1, II.20.1, VII.11.2, VIII.27.10, Strabo VII.4.8.
[11] Dem. IX.57-58, 66, etc.
[12] XVIII.14.

knave from Macedonia'.[13] He forgets that when they felt it necessary both Sparta (during the Peloponnesian War and later) and the Athenians (during the Corinthian War) had made use of even Persian help in their own interests against other Greeks. This is not to say that Demosthenes was mistaken in using such tactics in order to raise support for his point of view; just that we must not allow ourselves to be limited by such partisan viewpoints.[14]

Thirdly, what was Philip's attitude to Greece? Did the Macedonian, in spite of the strategic necessities of his confrontation of Greece, genuinely admire and respect the civilization and culture of the Greek people? His penchant, like some of his predecessors, for attracting skilled soldiers, entertainers and advisers to his court might suggest so.[15] His patent unwillingness to be drawn into war with Athens between 346 and 340 may be interpreted in this light. The leniency of his treatment especially of Athens after the Battle of Chaeronea admits of this interpretation. But beyond all these—all of which may be seen from another point of view[16]—there is the settlement of the Greek question by means

[13] Dem. IX.30.
[14] Cf. Loeb, *Demosthenes*, Vol. II, introductory note to Index, p. 475, explaining the omission of certain names from the Index: 'The traitors [named by Demosthenes at XVIII.295] we have allowed to remain in deserved obscurity', and compare Polybius XVIII.14.1-4ff.
[15] The strong, indeed overriding Greek influence revealed by the current excavations at Pella lends support to this, although what has so far been unearthed dates from early Hellenistic onwards. Building foundations, streets, drainage, mosaics, statuettes, and so on, are all very Greek.
[16] In advancing the objection that he wanted the co-operation of Greece for his projected invasion of Persia, it must be remembered that by his death he had given no indication of the extent of his plans; he may indeed have intended no more than an expedition into Asia Minor for the purpose of restocking his treasury, which seems to have been much depleted by the end of his reign; Arr.VII.9.6. But even on the assumption that he aimed at the empire as a whole (and we may doubt whether even Alexander intended so much before his early successes in Asia Minor), there seem to be only two possible reasons for seeking such co-operation, to avoid a mass uprising behind his back and to ensure the use of Greek soldiers and the Athenian navy. As far as the first is concerned, it seems probable that the only way to ensure harmony in Greece in his absence was to weaken it drastically by one of the methods suggested below. Second, for soldiers, all he needed was to spend the money he paid League of Corinth soldiers or mercenaries. The question of naval support is the most vital, but even here qualifications must be made. The Athenian navy may have been essential to him, but here again the main prerequisite would have been money; it is difficult to see what control over the rowers the leaders of a conquered and garrisoned Athens could have exercised against the attractions of generous wages and a share in the spoils. I see no reason to suppose that it was not a safer alternative to take the Athenian ships and pay for good crews, rather than relying on the loyalty of an Athenian people un-bloody as well as unbowed, but *see* Griffith, *G&R* 1965, 126-7.

General Introduction

of the League of Corinth. This 'common peace'[17] for all that it could have been dominated by Philip, had he lived, for all that at least some Athenians objected to it, and for all that the Greeks had no reasonable alternative but to agree to it, was, it seems, the most obvious way in which Philip showed a surprising degree of philhellenism. He could have kept Greece under far more effective control. He might have destroyed strategic points, such as Thebes, Corinth, Delphi, etc.; he might have split concentrations of population in the important areas, as had been done with Phocis;[18] he might have slaughtered or sold into slavery vast numbers of Greek soldiers.[19] Instead of doing such violence to the most cherished ideals and products of the Greek *polis*, he chose a settlement that, so it seems, was as far as possible in keeping with the Greek notion of autonomy, even though some of the alternatives might have allowed him a greater security of control.[20]

But this is not the whole picture. The policy of Demosthenes did not exist as a separate entity; it was initiated at a certain point in time and was formulated as a result of certain circumstances—circumstances not only of Philip's advance but also of the orator's career. While it is true to say that the advancement of Demosthenes' career made his opposition to Philip all the more effective, it is also clear that his opposition to Philip—and, so far as we can see, from the extant speeches, only this one policy—served to advance his career to the stage where he had as much influence in Athens as perhaps only Pericles had had before. He proclaimed his violently anti-Macedonian policy at a time when others were preoccupied with less extreme policies, and it is finally perhaps a matter of opinion whether Philip's local expansion in the earlier years justified this line or whether, conversely, this line itself provoked Philip's later expansion to the extent that it had reached by 338. But opinion or not, the latter view is at least tenable and if it has received almost no attention to date this is largely because of reliance on the evidence of one man. And whether the reader accepts this and other suggestions made here, rejects them or finds acceptable compromises, this book may serve its purpose; as I have said, our aim has been not to provide answers but to collect evidence sufficient for the reader to reach his own conclusions.

Finally, it will be obvious that the events and ideas contained in this small 'slice of history' can be studied properly only in context. Demosthenes' speeches are not only the product of the confrontation

---

[17] On which cf. Ryder, Chapter VII, and Roebuck, *CPh* 1948, 73-92.
[18] DS XVI.60.2.
[19] All of which possibilities would have avoided the need for large-scale deployment of occupation-troops, the obvious difficulty in another alternative, an effective network of garrisons.
[20] On the details of the 338 settlements, Roebuck, *CPh* 1948, 73-92.

The Spectre of Philip

of two men or two countries; they also reflect the effects of such factors as Greek weakness stemming ultimately from the Peloponnesian War,[21] the rise of mercenaries to prominence in the fourth-century style of warfare,[22] the influence of a severely troubled Persia, whose concern over her internal dissension led her more than ever to attempt to control the balance of power in Greece,[23] and the revival of Athenian imperialism—if rather toned down in comparison to that of the fifth century.[24] Macedonia seen over our period will be incomprehensible without the background of such factors as the part Philip played in the growth of the Macedonian state,[25] the organization of the army and its relevance to Macedonian society,[26] and Philip's attitude to Persia.

---

[21] Cf., for example, *CAH* VI, Chapters II,IV; Ryder, *Koine Eirene*, Chapters I-V.
[22] On which Parke, *Greek mercenary soldiers* . . ., is still the authoritative work.
[23] Ryder, Chapters I-V.
[24] Marshall, *The Second Athenian Confederacy*; Accame, *La lega ateniese*.
[25] *CAH* VI, 203ff., Griffith, *G&R* October 1965, 125-39; Hogarth, *Philip and Alexander of Macedon; two essays in biography*; Cloché, *Histoire de la Macédoine*, pp. 132-61.
[26] Griffith, *G&R* October 1965, 125-39; *PCPhS* 1956/7, 3,10.

LIBANIUS' INTRODUCTION TO THE SPEECHES OF DEMOSTHENES[1]

§1 Best of proconsuls, Montius,[2] you, like Asteropaios in Homer[3] being skilled in rhetorical matters, are the foremost figure in the Roman tongue and by general consent have carried off the first prize for culture among the Romans. Nor do you neglect the Greek tongue, insomuch as you are able to excel in it because of the greatness of your natural endowments. Indeed you spend time on all the orators, but especially on the most perfect of the Greek speakers, Demosthenes. Moreover, it was your wish that I should append for you a written introduction to his speeches. Gladly then do I accept your command (for I know that it is more of an honour than a labour) and I shall begin the composition with the orator's life, not recounting it in its entirety, for that would be too much, but mentioning only as much as seems to contribute also to a better understanding of the speeches.

§2 The father of Demosthenes the orator was Demosthenes, who appears to be unassailable in his birth, as is also testified by Aeschines, the orator's enemy. At any rate Aeschines used these very words: 'His father was Demosthenes from the Paianian deme, a man of free birth—for there is no need to falsify the facts'.[4] He possessed a factory of slaves who were knife-makers, from which he received the name 'Knife-maker'.[5] It is said however that the orator's ancestry on his mother's side was not pure Attic.[6] For his grandfather Kylon[7] went into exile from Athens on a charge of treachery and took up residence near the Black Sea. There he married a woman of Scythian race, from whom was born Kleoboule, the mother of Demosthenes. At any rate this has been made an object of abuse by many people, especially Aeschines, who said that he was a Scythian, a barbarian who had adopted Greek speech.[8]

---

[1] Written in AD 352 in Constantinople; RE XII.2522.
[2] Proconsul in AD 352.
[3] *Iliad* XII.102, XVI.351-352.
[4] Aes. III.171; cf. II.93. For D.'s family, XXVII.4.
[5] Aes. ibid., Dem. XVII.1 *et passim;* Plut. *Dem.* IV.1.
[6] Aes. II.171, 23, 78, 180, 183.
[7] Plut. *Mor.* 844A; Aes. II.171-172; also Dem. XXVIII.1-2.
[8] *See* Aes. II.78, III.171f., etc. So did Diogenes the Cynic, Plut. *Mor.* 847F, and the orator Dinarchus, I.15; cf. also Dem. LVII.30.

The Spectre of Philip

§3 So much then for his ancestry. When he was left an orphan by his father he was extremely young,[9] so it is said, and was physically weak and prone to illness,[10] so that he did not frequent the wrestling-school as all the male children of Athens were accustomed to do. As a result, when he had reached manhood he was mocked by his enemies for effeminacy and gained the nickname 'Batalos'.[11] It has been recorded that a certain Batalos was a flute-player from Ephesus and was the first to wear women's shoes on the stage and to indulge in effeminate practices; in general he made the art soft and effeminate. It was after him that dissolute and unmanly people were called 'Batalos'.

§4 Demosthenes is said to have gained his great and ardent passion for oratory from the following incident.[12] Callistratus was an Athenian orator of high repute. He was, so men say, about to contest a public law-suit, the one concerning Oropus I think. Demosthenes was then a boy and he begged the slave that had charge of him to allow him to go to the trial. The slave gave his permission. After hearing Callistratus Demosthenes was so inspired that from that time onwards everything took second place to oratory. As a teacher he had Isaeus, a very clever rhetorician.[13] On attaining his majority he immediately set in process a court-case against his guardians,[14] who had administered his property fraudulently. He secured their conviction but was unable to recover all that was lost. §5 Some say that the speeches against his guardians are by Isaeus and not Demosthenes. Their grounds for distrust are the orator's age, since he was only 18 years old when he brought the law-suits against them, and the fact that the speeches appear somewhat to display the style of Isaeus.[15] Others believe that they were composed by Demosthenes but revised and corrected by Isaeus. But it is not surprising that Demosthenes was able, even at that age, to compose such speeches—his later surpassing excellence adds credibility to this—and that as a result of his still-recent training under Isaeus he imitated his style in many ways. After these court-cases, when he had grown a little older, he tried to become a teacher of political philosophy; then, dropping this, he

---

[9] Plut. *Mor.* 844A.
[10] Plut. *Dem.* IV.3; Aes.III.255.
[11] Plut. *Dem.* IV.4; *Mor.* 847E; Aes. I.131. He was also nicknamed 'Argas', the name of a venomous snake, Aes. II.99; Plut. *Dem.* IV.5.
[12] Reported by Hegesius of Miletus *via* Plut. *Mor.* 844BC, where the incident is said to have taken place in the assembly. Plut. *Dem.* V connects the story with the trial over Oropus, which however did not take place until 366.
[13] Plut. *Mor.* 844C; also 837D, 839E for a probably unfounded connection with Isocrates, and Plut. *Dem.* V.5 for some other versions.
[14] 364/3 BC Plut. *Dem.* VI.1-2; *Mor.* 844CD; D.'s speeches XXVII, XXVIII, XXIX; XXX and XXXI follow in 362 as a direct result of the earlier trials.
[15] This is so; in fact, one passage is borrowed very nearly verbatim from Isaeus (compare XXX.37 with Isaeus VIII.12). Cf. also Plut. *Dem.* V.4-5.

Libanius' Introduction to the Speeches of Demosthenes

became an advocate in the courts. Having used these cases as what one might call a training-ground, he turned to popular oratory and participation in the political life of the city.

§6 The following facts may also be mentioned: that nature had given him a halting tongue and that he was somewhat weak in his breathing. The result of both these things was that his delivery was very poor and hence, at first, he did not gain a reputation for his oratory.[16] Because of this, when someone asked him 'In what does rhetoric consist?', he replied 'Delivery'; for he was aggrieved that because of his delivery he appeared worse than his inferiors.[17] But these faults he corrected by practice, as well as all the other deficiencies with regard to public speaking that were in him. For at first he was a coward in the face of the clamour and uproar of the crowd, and easily terrified, so that he immediately shrank away.[18] For this reason, they say, he kept watch for a violent wind and a rough sea and then declaimed as he walked along the shore; and by means of the roaring of the sea he accustomed himself to putting up with the barracking of the crowd.[19] §7 It is also said of him that he used to have underground chambers and to shave himself unevenly, in order that shame might stop him going out of doors,[20] and that he did not sleep even during the night but toiled on over his oratory till dawn. It was because of this that Pytheas, in mocking jest, said that Demosthenes' speeches smelt of the lamp.[21] Demosthenes' reply was both witty and cutting: 'I am aware that my lucubrations distress you', he said. For Pytheas had been maliciously slandered as indulging in armed robbery by night. Moreover, that he habitually drank water,[22] that he might the better keep his mind alert and wide-awake, has found universal agreement. We have also received the following story: that there was a time when he hung a sword from the roof, then, standing beneath it, would declaim. He did this because in his declaiming he had the habit of waving his shoulder in an unseemly manner, so he hung the sword above the shoulder, touching his skin. Thus, because he was afraid of being struck by the sword he was able to restrain himself in a seemly posture.[23]

§8 I must also describe to you how the affairs of the Greeks and the Athenians stood when Demosthenes entered upon his career of public

[16] Ibid., VI.3-VII.1; *Mor.* 844F.
[17] Plut. *Dem.* VII.2, XI.2-6; *Mor.* 845AB.
[18] See note 17 above.
[19] Plut. *Mor.* 844E.
[20] Plut. *Dem.* VII.3-VIII.1.
[21] Ibid., VIII.3-4.
[22] Dem. VI.30, XIX.46.
[23] Plut. *Mor.* 844E.

speaking. The Thebans, in a battle at Leuctra in Boeotia,[24] had defeated the Spartans, who were ruling over Greece and possessed the greatest power. As a result the Thebans themselves obtained a position of strength and after a short time they made war on the Phocians.[25] The Phocians were a people whose 22 cities bordered on Boeotia. They seized the nearby temple of the Pythian Apollo and plundered it.[26] Therefore the Thebans made war upon them.[27] The Athenians were also engaged in war—the so-called Social War[28]—for the Chians, Rhodians and the Byzantines, who were formerly Athenian subjects, had at that time formed a coalition and made an alliance and were at war with Athens. Thus Greece was divided into many parts—the Athenians at war with the people mentioned above, the Thebans with the Phocians and the Spartans with the Peloponnesians.[29] §9 At this time Philip son of Amyntas came to the Macedonian throne.[30] Amyntas the Macedonian king[31] had three children by the Illyrian Eurydice. Of these the eldest, Alexander,[32] met his end by assassination, the second, Perdiccas,[33] while fighting against the Illyrians. Philip, the youngest, was a hostage in Thebes when he learned of Perdiccas' death.[34] He slipped away in secret, came speedily to Macedonia and seized the throne.[35] The Athenians, with a great number of soldiers, tried to restore to the kingdom another man,[36] who was of the royal family but in exile from Macedonia. Philip attacked these and defeated them in battle. All the Athenian prisoners that he took he dismissed without ransom, not because of goodwill towards the city but because he had a generous disposition....[37]

[24] 371 BC; DS XV.53-56, etc.
[25] The Sacred War; for dates see Hammond, *JHS* 1937, 53-78.
[26] At Delphi; DS XVI.23.1.
[27] Ibid., 25.1.
[28] 357-355 BC; ibid., 7.3-4, 21.1-22.2. Libanius' chronology is out; the Social War had finished before the Sacred War began (Hammond, *JHS* 1937, 53-78, and Cawkwell, *C&M* 1962, 34-49).
[29] Dem. XVI *passim*.
[30] 359 BC; DS XVI.2.4.
[31] 393-384 and again 382-370.
[32] 370-369.
[33] 365-359; the interim reign of Ptolemy and Eurydice, 369-365, is ignored; DS XVI.2.4.
[34] Philip was in Thebes probably between 368 and 365, for as little time as eighteen months (Aymard, *REA* 1954, 15-36); cf. Beloch III.1.182 with refs; Pickard-Cambridge, *CAH* VI, 204, is probably correct in claiming that Philip held administrative posts in Macedonia between 365 and 359.
[35] Justin VII.5.9f. says he was appointed regent for the infant Amyntas IV (cf. *IG* VII.3055, *ll.* 7-8).
[36] Argaios; DS XVI.2.6, 3.3-6.
[37] At this point the manuscript breaks off.

PHILIPPIC I

Speech IV

PREFACE TO SPEECH IV[1]

Philippic I is the first act of the drama of Demosthenes and Philip. The orator, after beginning his career in support of Eubulus, that is, in support among other things of the policy of non-intervention in affairs outside the direct sphere of Athenian interest, has recently begun to move away from his previous loyalty.[2] After the Social War (357-355 BC), with the humiliating and costly defeat at the hands of her ex-allies, who had been aided by Mausolus of Caria and towards the end by the ultimatum of the Persian king, Athens' primary task was one of financial recuperation. This was the first aim of Eubulus and was obviously accepted by the Athenian people. Expeditions into the northern Aegean were too few and too half-hearted to achieve any purpose. However, when Athens was directly threatened by Philip's advance to Thermopylae in midsummer 352 she acted quickly and without hesitation: a force was sent, arriving before Philip and forcing him to choose between pitched battle against a superior position and retreat. He chose the latter.

Three important events took place between midsummer 352 and the delivery of *Philippic* I. First, after his rebuff at Thermopylae, Philip marched to Thrace, across to its eastern seaboard on the Propontis. His progress through Thrace may not have been direct but it was certainly achieved in a short time. He began a siege of Heraion Teichos, a fortified town some twelve miles from Perinthus, with the aid of two new allies, Perinthus and Byzantium, both former members of the Second Athenian League (until the Social War). Although this was

[1] The points made in this preface have been documented in the notes to the speech itself. It was thought unnecessary to duplicate references here, except to certain broader issues.
[2] As can be seen from an examination of his earlier speeches; cf. Jaeger, pp. 57ff., 70, 73, 76-7.

The Spectre of Philip

probably only a part of a broader plan to establish control in Thrace (Dem. I.13, tells us that he expelled some Thracian chiefs and installed others), it might also have been intended and was certainly seen in Athens as a direct threat to the main Athenian interest in the north—the Chersonese—important for the security of the Black Sea corn-route, on which Athens depended.[3] Second, after his Thracian campaign, Philip marched into Chalcidice, where he seems to have given the Olynthians and their allies an abrupt warning not to persist with their overtures of peace towards Athens. This may have been no more than a demonstration of power; Theopompus, in an uncertain reference, perhaps suggests this. But the only other source, Demosthenes (I.13), says: '. . . immediately (after recovering from his illness in Thrace) he attacked Olynthus'. (This may be read: '. . . he took the Olynthians in hand'; at any rate it certainly indicates a definite act of interference.) The third event, which may have begun a little earlier,[4] was the change in Demosthenes' policy. This was probably at least partly influenced by the first two, but another motive suggests itself: quite simply the beginning of the young man's attempts to rise to prominence in Athens.

No one who takes the view that *Philippic* I and the *Olynthiacs* mirror Demosthenes' attempts to discredit Eubulus and thus push himself forward need feel unduly cynical.[5] *Philippic* I, as we have pointed out in the notes, urges a military force that has virtually no chance of being approved and a strategy that is quite impracticable, not to say suicidal. With a man of Demosthenes' intelligence, such proposals are incomprehensible unless we assume that perhaps he did not expect approval. The speech, perhaps, is part of a plan to establish for himself a reputation as a powerful speaker on inflammatory issues, the type of reputation that will win for him the admiration of the bulk of the people—to whom, as in any age, a speaker who handles contentious issues in black-and-white terms will appeal (though, of course, not necessarily to the extent that they will commit suicide or throw money away by approving his wildest proposals). A further consideration is that at this time Demosthenes' main source of income is undoubtedly his work as a

---

[3] Cf. Dem. XX.31-32; Jones, pp. 77-8. Of secondary importance was Amphipolis, founded by Athens in 437 on the earlier Thracian site, Ennea Hodoi, but lost to the Spartan Brasidas in 424. After Cleon's unsuccessful attempt to recover it in 422, it was ceded back to Athens by the Peace of Nicias, but in spite of Athenian and, later, Chalcidian attempts to capture it, Amphipolis retained its independence. Athenian aspirations did not wane however and in spite of a vindication of Athenian rights over it in 371 (Aes. II.32), the many attempts in the 360s to assert these rights were failures. Nevertheless the Athenians continued to assert their claim (cf. below, II.6, I.5, 8, V.14, 25, with refs; also Isoc. *Philippus*).

[4] *See* refs to Jaeger, above.

[5] Cf. most recently Cawkwell, *CQ* 1962, esp. 134-40.

Preface to Speech IV

logographos, a composer of legal argument, which depends to a large degree on his being known as a skilful and persuasive rhetorician.[6]

By his actions at Thermopylae, Heraion Teichos and Olynthus, Philip gave Demosthenes his opportunity.[7] In his earlier public speeches the orator's fears were of the Persian king and of Sparta; now Philip has given him a more tangible fear to play upon. That the Athenians as a whole, however, did not yet see any necessity to act on his urging is clear enough; no force was voted, and even in 349/8 when Demosthenes had something considerably more tangible for motivation—the attack on Chalcidice—the help voted was far from what he advocated.

It was not until 6 or more years later that Demosthenes' ground-work was rewarded, when the Athenian disillusionment over the peace with Philip (the Peace of Philocrates, 346) caused the Athenians to turn, unwisely as it turned out, to the man who had urged, after the Peace and in the years before it, a policy of non-compromise. In the years after about 343 Demosthenes became Athens' most influential citizen; his policy of the late 350s and early 340s had borne fruit.

DATE[8]

The date of *Philippic* I has been disputed.[9] Recently Dionysius of Halicarnassus, who puts it at 352/1 (*ep. ad Amm.* IV), has found support, although qualified.[10] But for several reasons this is to be doubted. First, we may justly suspect Dionysius' source, particularly in this case, because he claims that the speech as we have it was actually two speeches (§§1-29 and §§30-51), the second delivered in 347/6. This assertion is now unanimously rejected. Without supporting evidence there is no reason to assume that he must be any more correct in his information on what he calls the first part of the speech.

It is generally conceded that the speech was delivered after Philip's advance to Thermopylae, his illness in Thrace and his attack on

---

[6] *See* my Appendix, 'Table of Extant Genuine Speeches of Demosthenes to 341' for an analysis of the types of D.'s speeches. It is plain that, around 355, his ambitions begin to show. Not only does he enter the political arena, but, between 355 and the end of his career, he writes only one more purely private speech (that is, of those that were published and are now extant). All the others are appeals (to what would now be a higher court) or cases involving offences against the State (which had to be prosecuted on its behalf by individuals). All of these, probably more lucrative, certainly attracted more attention (Kennedy, pp. 214-15).

[7] But note that these incidents took place before D.'s speech XV, which nevertheless contains only the briefest and most off-hand reference to Philip (XV.24).

[8] For a documented expansion of the following argument *see* Ellis, *REG* 1966, 636-9.

[9] Cf. Cawkwell, *CQ* 1962, 122-7, for bibliography and a more recent view.

[10] Ibid., and Sealey, *REG* 1955, 81-9.

Olynthus. The advance to Thermopylae came in midsummer 352, followed shortly by the Thracian campaign. The calculation of the length of the latter hangs on a rather ambiguous account in *Olynthiac* III (§§4-5 and note). The consequence of our interpretation of this is that Philip did not fall ill until September or October 351, at which point his Thracian campaign ended. He must, therefore, have made his Chalcidian attack later than that. At some date after the last, *Philippic* I was delivered (probably not immediately; there is no sign of immediacy in Demosthenes' references to Olynthus). Thus, a date of about January 350 is proposed for the speech.

LIBANIUS' INTRODUCTION TO SPEECH IV

The Athenians are faring badly in the war against Philip and they have come together in a mood of dejection. The speaker therefore attempts to put an end to their poor spirits, saying that it is not at all surprising that they have been beaten; it is due to their indifference.[1] He explains to them how they can best deal with the war. He bids them fit out two forces, a large one, composed of citizens, which will remain at Athens and remain ready to meet the needs of the moment,[2] and a smaller one,[3] where the men on active service will be mercenaries, but with an admixture of citizens alongside them.[4] This force, the speaker urges, is not to remain at Athens, nor to make its relief-expeditions from the city; it is to operate all around Macedonia and to carry on incessant warfare, so that there may be on Philip's very doorstep a force to oppose him,[5] and so that he may not make his assaults on affairs in the north by awaiting the onset of the Etesian winds or the winter (when sailing from Athens to Macedonia is impossible) and thus gain a complete control there during the Athenians' absence.[6]

---

[1] §§2-12.
[2] §§16-19.
[3] §§19-23, 28-29, etc.
[4] §21.
[5] This small force, as Libanius does not seem to realize, is far too small to have much effect, except, as D. says, in guerrilla-attacks; it can only flee from real opposition (§23). Further, is Philip sufficiently dependent on his coast to be seriously inconvenienced by these attacks? Cf. §32 and note.
[6] §§31-33. Libanius, like D., makes this important and valid point without acknowledging that it ought also to apply to the proposal for the larger force, which is to be stationed unmanned at Athens (note 2, above).

TRANSLATION AND COMMENTARY
Philippic I–c. January 350(?)

§1 Men of Athens, if some new topic were being proposed for discussion, I would have held back until most of the regular speakers had disclosed their views;[1] and then, if I were satisfied with anything they said, I would have held my peace, and if I were not satisfied, I would have tried to put forward my own point of view. But, since it so happens that the present debate is concerned with matters that these regular speakers have discussed many times, I think that I may reasonably be excused for standing up to speak first of all; for had these men given the requisite advice in the past[2] there would be no need for your deliberations now.[3]

§2 Firstly then, men of Athens, you must not be despondent at the present state of affairs even though they seem to be in a pretty bad way. For the aspect of the situation in the past that is worst is, in fact, the aspect that holds out most hope for the future. And what is this? It is the fact that your affairs are in an evil plight *because* you do none of the things that duty imposes on you; whereas if you were doing all you

---

[1] D.'s apparent modesty here may be due to one or both of two factors (a) it is probably a reference to the old Solonian ordinance allowing the oldest and most experienced to speak first in the assembly, but which by the fourth century had passed out of existence as a law, though it remained as an orderly but not invariable custom. Aeschines (III.2, 4) gives the origin and fate of the law, and (II.108) an example of the same principle under different circumstances (on an official embassy) and D. (XVIII.170, 191) gives the official contemporary invitation to speakers, 'Who wishes to speak?' Cf. also Jones, pp. 110-11; (b) D. may also be acknowledging his inexperience on matters of policy; he has, to date, and to our knowledge, delivered only three public speeches: *On the Navy Boards, For the Megalopolitans,* and *On the Freedom of the Rhodians.*

[2] D. takes up cudgels with the party of Eubulus, which had not, he now thinks, prosecuted the war against Philip with sufficient vigour. Cf. *CAH* VI, 222-5, Cawkwell, *JHS* 1963, 43ff., and Beloch III.1.343, 451, 484.

[3] Cf. Isocrates' proem to his *Archidamus* (§§1-2), which seems to have influenced Demosthenes, but which, in spite of its rhetorical opening in the manner of a young man, was actually a pamphlet composed by Isocrates at the age of 70. See *also* the introduction to the speech in Loeb, *Isocrates,* Vol. I, p. 344, Blass III.1.214, 219, 301, II.289.

Translation and Commentary: Philippic I

ought and they were still in such a state, there would be no hope of their improving. §3 Again, it must be borne in mind, both by those hearing the story from others and by those having first-hand knowledge as they recall the occasion, how strong and powerful the Spartans were only a short time ago, yet how nobly and befittingly you did nothing unworthy of the city, but undertook, in defence of the cause of justice, the war against them.[4] And why do I say this? So that you may look and see that when you are on your guard there is nothing that can alarm you, but when you let things slide nothing is the way you would wish it to be. Take as an example to prove this the might of Sparta at that time[5] and the wanton violence of Philip at the present; the former you overcame because you gave your attention to affairs of state, while the latter is throwing us into confusion[6] because we have no concern for the things that matter.

§4 And if anyone thinks that Philip is a tough opponent, as he considers the size of Philip's available resources[7] and the fact that our city has lost all her territories,[8] then he thinks rightly, though he should consider this: that there was a time when we had Pydna, Potidaea and Methone,[9] with all the surrounding area, well disposed towards us, and that many of the tribes that are now with him were then free and autonomous[10] and preferred to be on good terms with us rather than

---

[4] A reference to Athenian opposition to Sparta in the years 378-371 (Tod Nos 123, 131, *ll.* 37ff., Dem. XXII.15, Marshall, pp. 12-13, 16-18, *et al.*); that is, 20-odd years before.

[5] That is, before the Battle of Leuctra (371).

[6] Cf. §2 and Preface to this Speech.

[7] By the end of 351, Philip has reunited Macedonia (DS XVI.2.5-3.6), has at least gained influence, not to say power, in Thessaly (Sordi, Chapter IX), both tremendous sources of manpower and cavalry, and has probably carried out schemes of reorganization for the control of Thrace (Dem. I.13). In general, see *CAH* VI.203-21.

[8] He refers to Athenian allies, cleruchies and points of interest in the north lost to Philip before 350, Pydna and Methone (allies on Macedonian soil), Abdera and Maronea (bases on the Thracian south coast), Potidaea (a cleruchy in Chalcidice), Amphipolis (controlling the Pangaean mines of south-western Thrace) and Pagasae and Pherae (of strategic importance, the former providing an advance base for an attack on Athens and the latter guarding the landward approaches to Pagasae), and to the many allies lost through the Social War of 357-355 (for date and some comments cf. Cawkwell, *C&M* 1962, 34-49; on the war and subsequent loss of allies, Marshall, pp. 109-18, *CAH* VI, 209-12; Isocrates *On the Peace* is a reflection of Athenian disillusionment after the war). Cf. also Isoc. *Areopagiticus* 9, and Sealey, *JHS* 1955, 74-81.

[9] Cf. note 8 above. Pydna was lost in 356, Potidaea in the middle of that year, Methone in 354; DS XVI.8.3-5, 31.6, 34.4-5; Hammond, *JHS* 1937, 57-8, 67, 75.

[10] Cf. I.23 and note.

The Spectre of Philip

him. §5 If Philip at that time had formed the opinion that waging war on Athens was a hard and difficult task, since the city possessed so many fortresses in his own territory[11] and he himself was without allies, he would never have done any of the things he has now achieved, nor would he have won such great power. But, men of Athens, Philip saw full well that all these places are the prizes of war, ready for the taking, and that the possessions of those who are absent naturally belong to those on the spot, the possessions of the neglectful to those who will endure toil and danger. §6 This is his attitude and because of it he has subdued and possesses all the places in question. Some he now holds by right of conquest, others he has brought into alliance and friendship;[12] for all men are prepared to ally themselves and give attention to those whom they see are ready and willing to do what should be done. §7 Men of Athens, if you are ready to put yourselves in such a frame of mind as this now—for, to date, you have not been—and if each one of you puts aside all his shilly-shallying and shows himself ready to act where he ought to act and where he could be of use to the city (that is, the man with money must pay the property-tax and the man of military age must go on active service);[13] if, I say, to sum up plainly and briefly, you will agree to become your own masters and will cease, each one of you, from expecting to do nothing yourself and your neighbour to do everything on your behalf, then you will redeem what is your own, you will recover what you have let slip through your own carelessness and you will take your revenge upon Philip.[14]

§8 For you must not regard his present position as being invested with an eternal immutability, as though he were a god; he is hated, feared and envied, even by some of the people who now appear to be

[11] Precisely the reason why Philip at least embarked on his aggressive policy.
[12] It must have galled the Athenians to see former allies of importance, such as Byzantium and Perinthus, now in alliance with Philip, in fact helping against Athenian interests at Heraion Teichos in 351 (Tod No. 123, Isoc. *Philippus* 53, Dem. V.25, Isoc. *On the Peace* 16; for the participation of Byzantium and Perinthus, schol. Aes. II.81, Marshall, p. 118; Pickard-Cambridge, p. 179).
[13] For details of what was involved in an *eisphora* (property-tax or war-tax) and in military service *see* Jones, pp. 23-33. An important point that may be raised here is the composition of D.'s audience. He is addressing himself to those who are qualified, on the basis of property and wealth, to serve in the citizen-force and to pay the war-tax; that is, a fair proportion, if not a majority, must be middle or upper middle class (cf. Jones, pp. 35-6, 75-96, Perlman, *Athenaeum* 1963, 327-55, esp. 335-6).
[14] This appeal to Athenians to overcome their apathy and to bear their responsibility in a practical manner is the theme of most of Demosthenes' policy-speeches and in particular of those delivered before the Peace of Philocrates (346). See, for example, Dem. I.6, 8, 9, 20, II.4, 11, 12, 13, III.10-12, 19, 34-36, IV.9, 11. The key to his argument is most clearly stated in II.4. Also cf. III.8-9 and note.

particularly well disposed towards him.¹⁵ And you must recognize that all the desires and emotions that other men have are present also in the people ranged on Philip's side, although they are all now repressed and have no outlet, thanks to your indolence and indifference—of which I urge you to rid yourselves immediately. §9 Look at the situation, men of Athens, and see what a peak of insolence the fellow has reached. He gives you no choice between action and living at peace, but threatens, utters arrogant statements—so it is said—and cannot be satisfied by his conquests, but is always seeking fresh acquisitions and trying to hedge us in on all sides, while we procrastinate and sit idly by. §10 Men of Athens, when will you do your duty? What must happen before you will do it? 'When' comes the reply, 'the need arises.' But how ought we to regard what is happening now? For my part, I think that for free men a sense of shame over the conduct of their affairs is the most compelling necessity of all. Or, tell me, are you content with going around asking one another: 'Is there any news?' Could there be any hotter news than a Macedonian beating Athenians in war and administering the affairs of the Greeks? §11 'Is Philip dead?' 'No, but he's ill!'¹⁶ What difference does it make to you? If he dies you will soon make yourselves another Philip, if this is the way you give your attention to your affairs. For Philip has not become great so much by his own strength as by our neglect. §12 And a further point: if anything happens to Philip, if our good fortune—which has always looked after us better than we look after ourselves—should bring this about, I would have you know that if you were close at hand you could take advantage of the general confusion and handle the situation as you wish. But as you now stand, you could not take over Amphipolis even if the opportunity was offered to you, for you are far from ready for it, both in your state of preparations and in your whole outlook.¹⁷

§13 Well then I'll say no more on this subject, since I think that you realize and are convinced that everyone must show himself ready and

---

[15] Cf. also I.5-6, 21-24, II.5-10. There is no evidence to suggest that by 350 the Macedonians or the Thessalians are dissatisfied. This may however be a reference to the Chalcidian overtures to Athens that were suppressed by Philip, 351; Dem. XXIII.108-109 notes the statement of Olynthian peace and desire for alliance with Athens; I.13, IV.17 and Theopompus F 127 (cf. our Appendix, 'Selection of Historical Fragments') mention Philip's intervention. Cf. also Sealey, *REG* 1955, 81-9, esp. 82. For the date, see the Preface to this Speech.

[16] It seems fairly certain from Demosthenes' choice of words here that the news of Philip's death or illness was in fact a real issue not long ago. This being so, we may date it from a later reference of D. (III.4-5) to about September or October 351, if our interpretation is correct (cf. my Appendix, 'Chronological Table' and I.13 with notes).

[17] By his stress on the need for a force on the spot, D. lays the ground-work for his proposal of a dual military force (§§16-37, etc.).

The Spectre of Philip

willing to do his duty.[18] Now therefore I shall try to tell you the type of military force I think could set us free from such a situation, what its size must be, what financial resources will be needed, and how I think all further preparations may best and most quickly be made. But first, men of Athens, I shall ask this much of you: pass judgement when you have heard all I have to say; don't try to pre-judge the issue. §14 And if anyone gets the impression at first that I am proposing a novel kind of military force, let him not think that I am trying to postpone operations.[19] It is not those who cry 'Quickly!' and 'Today!' who speak most to the point (for the expeditionary force we are now discussing will not prevent what has already been done); §15 it is the man who can demonstrate what military force can be provided, how big it is to be, and the means whereby it will be able to keep the field till such a time as we either consent to a settlement of the war or overcome our enemies. For this is the way for us to avoid further disasters in the future. Well then, I believe I can tell you these things, though I shall not stand in the way if someone else proposes a solution. My promise is thus a bold one, but it will soon be put to the test in action and you will be the judges.

§16 Firstly then, men of Athens, I say that we must fit out 50 triremes;[20] secondly, we must get it into our heads that, if the need arises, we have to embark and sail in them ourselves.[21] On top of this, I would have us make ready horse-carrying triremes for a half of the

[18] A rhetorical ploy. That the Athenians were *not* convinced by the force of his argument is evident from their lack of activity between 350 and 349/8 and from Demosthenes' own speeches in the latter year, the three *Olynthiacs*.

[19] D. means that because his proposal is to involve a striking-force which will need considerable organization he may be accused of delaying any action for the length of time the preparations will take. It is interesting to speculate on precisely what he did intend in view of the likely effectiveness of what he proposes (cf. Dem. III.4-5 and I.13 with notes; also the Preface to this Speech and my Appendix, 'Chronological Table'). Does the present admonition establish his bona fides or his skill in concealing his awareness of the impossibility of the whole scheme?

[20] D. appears to mean that these 50 ships would be fitted out by the trierarchs (cf. §36 and note) and then left unmanned at the Piraeus until such time as they are needed.

[21] The larger force, apparently, is to be manned, when it is needed, only by citizens. Two advantages of this plan would be (a) that citizens might conceivably be persuaded or compelled to serve on a mere allowance for provisions (cf. §28 and note) and to act as both hoplites and rowers, whereas mercenaries undoubtedly would not, and (b) that presumably a citizen-levy (cf. §21 and note) could be organized more quickly than mercenaries could be engaged. However, what D. does not acknowledge (cf. Libanius' Introduction to Speech IV, note 6) is that this potentially expensive force would suffer from the same weakness that D. wishes to avoid with the small force—its inability to reach the point of action in time to be effective (§§31-37, 39-41).

Translation and Commentary: Philippic I

cavalry and sufficient transport-ships.[22] §17 I think we ought to have these in readiness to counter Philip's sudden raids[23] from Macedonia towards Thermopylae, the Chersonese, Olynthus and wherever he wishes.[24] For we have to make him realize that you might perhaps rouse yourselves from your excessive negligence as you did when you made an expedition to Euboea and, so we are told, on a former occasion to Haliartus and most recently, only the other day, to Thermopylae.[25] §18 And, I might say in passing, such a force cannot be treated with complete contempt,[26] even if you do not do what I suggest—and I state that you must do it. Thus one of two things will happen: either Philip will know that you are prepared (and he will know full well; for, to be

[22] D. specifies only the 50 ships and, probably, 500 cavalry (one-half?—Jones, p. 81). However, his audience and certainly his opponents need only calculate briefly to realize that a force of 10,000 hoplites (at least) will be required (a) on the analogy of the small force and (b) to have any chance of being effective (cf. 17, 44; but also §50 and note).

Although we are not always sure what ships are used for transporting cavalry, D. here specifies (presumably converted) triremes. Thucydides mentions the first use of these (II.56 and Gomme II, p. 163) and in his account of the Sicilian expedition seems to put their capacity at 30 horses each (VI.43; the reference is not conclusive, as we do not know whether the ship was full to capacity, but a total of 30 horses with attendants, and 60 rowers, seems reasonable; for the number of rowers, *IG* II² 1628, col. b, *ll.* 154-155, 1627, col. b, *ll.* 241-265). Thus D.'s plan calls for about 14 cavalry-transports.

If the hoplites are not to row the 50 war-triremes, they will require up to 100 transports (following Kromayer and Veith, p. 184, on Thuc. VI.43) with 100 to 150 crew apiece. We might suggest a total potential cost of 400 to 650 talents per year (or 35 to 55 per month), depending on whether the hoplites are to row or not.

[23] If this force is to take effective action against Philip's 'sudden raids from Macedon . . .', it must surely be stationed in the northern Aegean. However, D. has already said (§16) that it is to be based at Athens, and we may suppose that although he must be aware of the likely ineffectiveness of what he is here proposing (cf. §§31-34, a reference apparently to the smaller force, but the point of which obviously applies to both), he also knows that to propose such an expensive (cf. §28 and notes) standing force in the north will be to provoke the ridicule of his opponents. Whatever the reason, the inconsistency will have been as obvious to his audience as it is to us.

[24] The speed of this succession of forays is stressed. Philip was at Thermopylae in midsummer 352 (DS XVI.38.1-2, Just. VIII. 2.8-12, Dem. XIX.84, XVIII.32, Hammond, *JHS* 1937, 57), in Thrace at Heraion Teichos only five months later (Dem. I.13, III.4-5), and, after nearly a year's campaign in Thrace, ended by his illness, he went immediately to Olynthus and its allied cities of the Chalcidian peninsula (cf. the Preface to this Speech and III.4-5 and notes).

[25] Euboea: 357 BC (DS XVI.7.2-3; also Loeb, *Diodorus Siculus*, Vol. VII, p. 255 n. 3, Dem. I.8, *CAH* VI, 207). Haliartus (in Boeotia): 395 BC (Xen. *HG* III.5.3-25, *CAH* VI, 46). Thermopylae: 352 BC (cf. note 24, above). 'Only the other day' is a rhetorical exaggeration.

[26] That is, in essence the scheme is sound, though details may need to be amended.

The Spectre of Philip

sure, there are those among our own citizen-body, more than there ought to be, who keep him fully informed)[27] and hold his peace through fear; or he will overlook these preparations and be caught off guard, since there will be nothing to stand in the way of your sailing against his country, if he gives you an opportunity.

§19 This, then, is the course of action I claim everyone should be resolved upon, and these are the preparations I think should be made. But before you do this, men of Athens, I say that you ought to make ready some sort of force that will wage war without a break and will do damage to Philip. And don't offer me 10 or 20,000 mercenaries nor these 'paper' forces of yours,[28] but one that will belong to the city and that will obey and follow its commander, whether you elect to this position one man or several, whether it is so-and-so or anyone you like. And you must provide maintenance for this force.

§20 What will this force be? How large will it be? Where will it find its sustenance? How will it be willing to do the things I suggest? I'll tell you, taking each question separately. As far as mercenaries are concerned—and please don't do what has too often caused you harm in the past; for, thinking that the utmost is too little for the occasion and deciding on the greatest enterprises in your decrees, you don't even do the small things when it comes to action.[29] Rather do the small things, make small provisions, then add to these if they are obviously too small. §21 Well then, I say that the total number of soldiers must be 2,000 and of these 500 must be Athenian citizens taken from whatever age-group you think fit[30] and serving in relays for a fixed period of time—not a lengthy period but only as long as you feel is right. The rest of the soldiers are to be mercenaries. Along with these there must be 200 cavalry, of whom at least 50 are to be Athenians;[31] they must serve in the same manner as the infantry. There must also be transport-vessels

[27] Although this aside may be inserted for its propaganda value, the charge of aiding Philip through information or more active help is one Demosthenes makes many times, notably in the *False Embassy* and *On the Crown* (cf. for example, XIX.8-13, XVIII.25-42).

[28] That is, those forces that look impressive when decided upon for their large numbers of ships but are ineffective because the State has not provided crews or money, leaving it to the commander to recruit troops with promises of booty. There were many examples of this during the Second Athenian League (Marshall, pp. 68, 71, etc. For the most recent example: Dem. III.4-5—if our interpretation is correct).

[29] Cf. note 28, above.

[30] The normal method for raising a levy was to call up (on a property basis) all those within a certain age-range, the range determined by the number of eligibles in it, allowing roughly for those in it who would be incapacitated in one way or another (Dem. III.4-5; Jones, pp. 79, 81-2).

[31] The reason for the admixture of mercenaries and citizens is explained in §§24-25.

Translation and Commentary: Philippic I

for the cavalry.³² §22 So far so good. But we must have in addition 10 fast triremes; Philip has a fleet,³³ so we too need fast triremes so that our force may sail in safety.³⁴ And where will we find the maintenance for these troops? I shall tell you that too and demonstrate it to you after I have shown why I feel that a force of this size is sufficient and why I say that the combatants must be citizens.

§23 I think, men of Athens, that the force must be this size for the following reason: we are not able to field a force that could take on Philip in a set battle; we must rather engage in guerrilla activities and employ this sort of warfare at first. Thus the force must not be too large—for there is neither pay nor sustenance for it—nor must it be absolutely weak. §24 And my reason for stating that citizens must be in the force and sail with it is that I hear that on a former occasion the city maintained a mercenary force at Corinth under the leadership of Polystratus, Iphicrates, Chabrias and others, and that you yourselves served along with it.³⁵ And I know from what I hear that you and the mercenaries, fighting side by side, defeated the Spartans in a set battle. But since mercenary forces have been conducting your campaigns all by themselves, they have continually beaten your friends and allies, while your enemies have grown stronger than they should.³⁶ The mercenaries take a quick look at the city's war then go sailing off to Artabazus³⁷ and

---

32 Although he specifies transports for the cavalry, he does not for the infantry. This does not mean that he intends the soldiers to act also as rowers; he could hardly engage mercenaries on such terms, especially in view of the low payment offered (§§28-29 and notes), and, in any case, he calculates the cost of the force on the basis of soldiers *and* rowers (§28). 2,000 soldiers will require 20 transports (§16 and note), involving another 2,000 or more rowers. That he has thus understated the cost will be apparent to his listeners.

33 Philip's fleet is probably small; its activities so far (§34 below) have been modest though effective. On the naval facilities open to Philip's use, cf. Grote, pp. 107-10.

34 As transport-ships are manned by considerably fewer rowers (100 to 150 in the case of troop-transports, 60 in that of cavalry-transports; §16 and note), they will travel a good deal more slowly than war-triremes under power of oars. Thus the advantage of the fast ships will be negated by the slowness of those they must convoy; the former can escape only by abandoning the latter.

35 During the Corinthian War of 394-387 (DS XIV.91-92 and Nepos *Iphic.* 2.3 for Iphicrates and Chabrias; Polystratus is unknown).

36 Parke, pp. 1-2, 125-32, 143. While D. is conscious of the failings of mercenaries, he is also aware that the old 'pre-mercenary' style of warfare is outmoded; IX.48.

37 Early in 355 Chares, the remaining Athenian commander in charge of the fleet directed against Byzantium, joined Artabazus' revolt against the Persian king. His aim was money, probably because he had not been voted sufficient for the projected siege (DS XVI.21-22.1, 34.1; also schol. Dem. I.19). The result: the enmity of the king, which became the major factor in the settling of the Social War to Athens' humiliation (Isoc. *Areop.* 8, 81).

anywhere else they please, while their commander follows them around —and not surprisingly because he can't give them orders if he doesn't give them pay.

§25 Therefore I maintain that you must remove the excuses of both the commander and the soldiers by providing pay and by setting your own soldiers as overseers of what is done on campaigns. For the way we handle things now is farcical. If someone should ask you: 'Are you at peace, men of Athens?' you would say indignantly: 'We certainly are not; we're at war with Philip.' §26 Yet are you not in the habit of electing from your number 10 regimental commanders, 10 general officers, 10 commanders of cavalry regiments and 2 general cavalry officers?[38] And what do these do? With the exception of the one man you send out to the war, the rest assist the *hieropoioi* to escort the sacred processions.[39] For you, like manufacturers of clay dolls, elect your regimental commanders and your cavalry officers for display in the *agora*, not for the war. §27 Surely, men of Athens, the regimental officers should come from your number; surely the cavalry commander should come from your number; surely the officers should be Athenian citizens, in order that the force may be really and truly a force of the city? Yet your own cavalry commander has to sail off to Lemnos[40] while Menelaus commands the troopers who are fighting to defend the city's possessions.[41] And I don't say this in disparagement of the man, but the cavalry commander, whoever he may be, should be a person elected by you.

§28 It may be that you think all I say is very true, but desire particularly to hear the financial side of the matter to learn how much it will cost and where the money will come from. So I shall go straight

---

[38] There were elected annually in Athens 10 general officers (*strategoi*), 10 *taxiarchoi* (each leader of a tribal infantry *taxis*), 10 *phylarchoi* (commanders of the tribal cavalry contingents), and 2 general cavalry officers called *hipparchoi*; Arist. *Ath.Pol.* 61. In earlier times when Athens was served by a full citizen-levy, where each of the tribes formed its own regiment, all these officers would be present (Hdt. VI.103-104, *et al.*), but later, when mercenaries formed a large proportion of the forces, three, two or often only one Athenian general was used. At Chaeronea there were two (DS XVI.85.2).

[39] Cf. Xen. *HG* I.4.20-21. For the four types of *hieropoioi*, or religious officials, at Athens see Roberts and Gardner, *An Introduction to Greek Epigraphy*, 2 vols, 1887-1905, Vol. II, p. 26 n. 9. Those here referred to by D. are probably officials whose function was to organize the Eleusinian Mysteries.

[40] Aristotle (*Ath.Pol.* 61.6) informs us that a cavalry-commander (apparently a third, not one of the two already mentioned) was regularly sent to Lemnos to command the cavalry there.

[41] Harpocration (*under* 'Menelaos') assumes this to be the half-brother of Philip, but it is probably the Menelaus of Pelagonia (in the hinterland of Macedonia) who is thanked in an Athenian inscription of 363/2 for his military and financial aid to Timotheus in Chalcidice; Isoc. *Antidosis* 111-113; Tod No. 143; and Marshall, p. 95.

Translation and Commentary: Philippic I

on and deal with this. As regards the money, the maintenance needed for this force—that is, the bare rationing[42]—amounts to 90 talents and a little besides; for 10 swift warships 40 talents are needed, at 20 minae per ship per month;[43] a similar amount is required for 2,000 soldiers,[44] so that each soldier may receive 10 drachmai per month ration allowance; for the cavalry, 200 in number, if each trooper receives 30 drachmai per month this comes to 12 talents;[45] §29 and if anyone thinks it slight provision to grant only their ration-money to the men serving in the force, then he is wrong. For I know full well that, if this is what happens, the force will itself provide the remainder from the war, without harming any of the Greeks or our allies, so that it will have its full pay.[46] If this is not the case I am prepared to sail with the expedition as a volunteer and to suffer the worst.[47] Where then will the money, which I maintain must come from you, be found? I shall explain right now.

[42] Rations, as distinct from pay.
[43] While it is difficult to be certain of rates of military pay for the fourth century, we may be certain that the rates proposed here are extremely low. For the fifth century cf. Thuc. III.17.4, V.47.6, VI.8.1, 31.3, VIII.45.2, Xen. HG I.5.5-7, V.2.21. In general for the fourth century, Parke, pp. 232-3, and Jones, pp. 31-2 with Dem. L.10, 12, 14, 23, 53; also Tod No. 183, whence it appears that Alexander's hypaspists were used as the standard for calculation of other rates of pay for soldiers serving the League of Corinth, CAH VI, 360 and Griffith, Mercenaries of the Hellenistic World, pp. 264-73. D.'s calculation here allows for a rate of 2 obols per day per rower. With 10 ships each carrying nearly 200 rowers earning 2 obols each for 360 days, the total, as he says, is 40 talents. (The normal Attic Year, that is, 5 out of every 8 years, had 354 days, the other 3, 384. Therefore 360 is a reasonable number for calculation, especially as there were 36,000 obols to the talent.)
[44] The same rate for soldiers as for rowers.
[45] For 200 cavalrymen, each paid 1 drachma per day for 360 days, the total is 12 talents per year. Cf. note 43, above; this rate too is extremely low when even a public slave was given 3 obols (one-half of a drachma) per day (Jones, p. 32). The total of 92 talents given by D. will actually be considerably short of the amount needed, which must include provision for the extra transports and their rowers (§§16, 22 and notes).
[46] An unduly optimistic statement after the experiences of the admirals of the Second Athenian League, who were often forced to obtain money from friend and foe alike in order to carry out their commissions, and, in one case, even to hire out a force of hoplites and rowers as agricultural labourers (Marshall, pp. 64-5, 67-70, 71, 76, 77, etc.). Compare this statement with §24. Griffith, Mercenaries . . ., pp. 271-3, interprets 'full pay' as implying that later, when Athens has received the profits of the war, the rations will be supplemented with the pay that was originally unpaid. This does not seem likely in the context; if, as D. is evidently conscious, potential soldiers—citizen or mercenary—are likely to jib at these rates, why not simply promise a later *fixed* supplement to the ration allowance? His very vagueness suggests that he is referring to profits from looting. In any case, as Griffith (p. 273) says, '. . . it left . . . too much to speculative hopes of the future and the fortunes of war . . .'
[47] D. is safe enough with this promise. In the first place, he is proposing to send

The Spectre of Philip

DEMONSTRATION OF SOURCES OF FINANCE[48]

§30 There then, men of Athens, are the results of the investigations of my friends and myself.[49] When you vote upon the motions, you will, if they please you, vote for these proposals, in order that you may make war upon Philip not only in your decrees and dispatches but also by your actions.

§31 It seems to me that your deliberations about the war and about the entire military preparation would be made on a better basis if you were to bear in mind the position of the country against which you are waging war and if you were able to take into account the fact that Philip gains most of his successes by using the winds and the seasons of the year to forestall us. He watches out for the Etesian winds or the winter, then he makes his attempt when we cannot reach the place.[50]

§32 You must bear these things in mind then and conduct the war not by means of special expeditions—for then we shall always be too late—but by means of a permanent military establishment and force. As a winter base for the force you can use Lemnos, Thasos, and Sciathos and the

---

the force with far too little money (§28 and notes); and second, his aim that the ships should be fast enough to avoid trouble is unlikely to be realized, owing to the presence of the slow transports (§22 and notes). What he is doing is proposing an impossible expedition to the very people who must pay for it and/or serve in it (§7 and note). Can he possibly expect approval? Cf. also Cawkwell, *Mnemosyne* 1962, 377-83, esp. 383 n. 1, who suggests that D. was advocating that the 92 talents come not from an *eisphora* (war-tax) but from normal revenues.

[48] At this point, according to D.Hal., *ep.ad Amm.* 4, 10, *Philippic* I ends; what follows, he says, was D.'s fifth *Philippic*, delivered after the three *Olynthiacs*. For literature on this question, cf. most recently Musurillo, *CQ* 1957, 86-7. Suffice it to note here that all modern editors reject D.Hal.'s claim (cf. for example, Blass III.1.304-5).

[49] The Greek does not say 'my friends and myself' but does use the plural pronoun. D. may mean that he has had help from some of the financial officers of the State (cf. Arist. *Ath.Pol.* 47-48) or merely from members of the same political group—unless this is a use of the 'royal plural'.

[50] The Etesian winds blow from the north-west during the months July to September in most years (Hdt. II.20), making it very difficult for a fleet to sail north from Athens. Poor weather conditions in the winter made sailing, especially in triremes, extremely hazardous (Adcock, p. 38). Consequently expeditions were delayed until the weather improved. To make matters worse, there was only a short time between the end of the Etesian winds and the onset of winter In §35 D. bewails the Athenian habit of arriving late on the scene, as at Methone, Pagasae, and Potidaea. In the case of Methone, at least, they were probably delayed by the Etesian winds (the date of Methone's fall was probably summer or autumn 354; Hammond, *JHS* 1937, 57-8). In 349/8 the third Athenian expedition to Olynthus was sent probably in June 348 but, because of these winds, did not arrive until Olynthus had fallen, three months later, in September; Cawkwell, *CQ* 1962, 130-4.

Translation and Commentary: Philippic I

islands in this area,⁵¹ on which there are harbours, food and everything necessary for an army. During the summer, when it is easy to stay close to land and the winds are safe, there will be no difficulty in the force's remaining hard by Philip's very country and the entrances to his trading-depots.⁵²

§33 The man you appoint commander of this force will decide according to circumstances how and when it will be used. What you must provide are the things I have written in my proposal. If you make these provisions, men of Athens, especially the money I speak of, and then after making ready the other things—the soldiers, the triremes and the cavalry—if you bind the entire force by law to remain at the seat of the war⁵³ (becoming yourselves the treasurers and providers of finance and exacting an account of his activities from the commander), then you will put an end to your habit of deliberating always about the same matters and doing nothing further about them. §34 In addition, you will deprive Philip of the most important of his sources of supply. What is this? The fact that he gets the revenues to wage war on you from your allies as he harries and plunders those sailing the seas.⁵⁴

---

⁵¹ Lemnos, long an Athenian cleruchy (Hdt. VI.137-140), had been abandoned at the end of the Peloponnesian War but later recovered, confirmation being secured under the terms of the King's Peace (Xen. HG V.1.31). Thasos, an Athenian dependency (Dem. VII.15, XII.2), formed the base of Athenian operations in the late 360s and early 350s against Amphipolis and was a stopping point on the corn-route (Dem. L.14, 21ff., 29, 46ff.). Sciathos was a subject-ally that because of its proximity to the Magnesian coast was particularly vulnerable to Philip (Dem. VIII.37). Others in that area subject to Athens were Skopelos, Halonnesos, and Peparethos.

⁵² Presumably with the intention, as perhaps in I.17-18, of ravaging Philip's coastline. Why? To disrupt his trade? Although we know little of Macedonian sea-trade at this time, we do know that the economy depended very little on overseas contacts and mainly on trade with neighbouring Chalcidice (West, NumChron 1923, 169-211, Arist. Econ. II 1350a.22 with Griffith, PCPhS 1956/7, 8). It is difficult to see how blocking what trading-depots there were could have had much if any effect.

⁵³ The argument (§§31-34) that to be effective the small force must be stationed in the north is valid. However, it is all the more applicable to the large force, the only one capable of withstanding Philip's 'sudden raids from Macedon' (§17 and note)—and D. must realize this. His large force will suffer from precisely those faults that he is pointing out here. Can he have been unaware of the contradiction? Can he have imagined that his audience would be unaware of it?

⁵⁴ That Philip's raids on enemy shipping provided him with his greatest resources is very doubtful. Beside the income from the Pangaean gold and silver mines (on which West, NumChron 1923, 169-211) and taxes of various kinds (presumably from the Macedonian people and others, such as the Thessalians, whose harbour and market dues went to Philip; Dem. I.22, II.11) any additional revenue from this source is not likely to be large. It suits D.'s argument here to exaggerate.

The Spectre of Philip

And a further point: you yourselves will be out of reach of harm from Philip. He will no longer be able to act as he has in the past when he burst in upon Lemnos and Imbros and departed with Athenian citizens as his prisoners,[55] when he seized the merchant fleet at Geraistos[56] and levied an incredible amount of money, and when, finally, he landed at Marathon and departed from the country taking the sacred trireme[57]— while you are not able to prevent him nor can you send an expedition which will arrive at the time you decide upon.

§35 And yet, men of Athens, why do you think the Panathenaic festival and the festival of Dionysus[58] always take place at the proper time, whether they have as superintendents experts or private citizens you have chosen by lot? On these festivals a greater amount of money is spent than on any of your expeditions, so that they have such a crowd of people, such a splendour of preparation as to be beyond compare. But your expeditions, on the other hand, are always behind the times—the one to Methone, to Pagasae, to Potidaea.[59] And why? §36 Because all matters concerned with these festivals are fixed by law and you each know long in advance who is *choregos* or *gymnasiarch* of his tribe,[60] what he must first receive, when and from whom, and then what he must do; none of these matters is neglected, none is left

---

[55] Since the early fifth century Lemnos and Imbros have belonged to Athens (Hdt. VI.137-140). Aeschines (II.72) mentions incidents perhaps similar to this in the period just before 346. For evidence of Macedonian policy, cf. note 67, below, and Androtion F 24 (Jacoby).

[56] Geraistos: a town on the southern tip of Euboea, vital, because of its position (Strabo X.444), to the Athenian corn-route. The merchant fleet referred to here will have been corn-ships returning to Athens.

[57] Cf. Dem. *Exordia* 21.3. Athens used 2 special triremes for religious and other special occasions (e.g., Thuc. VIII.73-74) as well as for dispatch-ships or flagships occasionally (Aes. III.162). The lesser known (to us) was the Salaminia (Thuc. III.33; later named Ammonias, at a date unknown but before the Arist. *Ath.Pol.* was written; ibid., 61.7). The other was the Paralos (Thuc. III.33, VIII.74, Dem. XXI.173, Poll. VIII.116, *IG* II² 1623, *ll.* 225ff., Ar. *Birds*, *l.* 1204), which, apparently, in the course of its annual mission in May to Apollo at Delos (Arist. *Ath.Pol.* 56) used to call at Marathon to offer sacrifice at the sanctuary of Apollo there.

[58] For details of these festivals, Daremberg-Saglio *under* 'Panathenaia' and 'Dionysia'; Deubner, *Attische Feste*, pp. 22-35, 138-42. The most recent and useful work on the former is Davison, *JHS* 1958, 23-42.

[59] Cf. §4 and notes; compare with §31. The only way to resolve these problems, if the war is to continue to the death, is to station a force in the north (§33).

[60] *Choregos*: one who performs the liturgy of the *choregia*; that is, he defrays the cost of and provides training for a chorus for a dramatic production in the Dionysia (Arnott, pp. 31, 53; Hdt. V.83; Antiphon VI.11; and Aes. I.11). *Gymnasiarchos*: performer of another of the liturgies, that of supervising the *palaistra* and paying the training-masters. In effect he fulfilled the same function for games as the *choregos* did for drama; Lys. XXI.3, Ps-Xen. *Ath.Pol.* 13, Arist. *Pol.* 1323a. On the cost of these liturgies Jones, pp. 55-7.

Translation and Commentary: Philippic I

unexamined, none is left vague and indefinite. But in matters concerning the war and in our preparations for it everything is disorganized, badly managed and vague. Because of this, we only appoint trierarchs after we have received a piece of news;[61] then we establish for them exchanges of property[62] and look into the sources of money for the expedition. After this we decide that the metics and the 'dwellers apart'[63] should embark on the ships; then that the crews should be citizens, then that we should put substitutes on board; §37 and while all this delay is going on, the object of the naval expedition, whatever it be, is already lost.[64] For we spend on preparation the time that should be spent on action, but the opportunities for action do not wait on our slowness and hesitation. As for the forces which we think we possess in the period between crises, these, when the crises occur, are shown to be incapable of doing anything. Philip, meanwhile, has reached such a pitch of arrogance that he is even now writing such letters as this to the Euboeans.

[READING OUT OF PHILIP'S LETTER][65]

§38 Men of Athens, of the things that have been read out the majority are true—and they ought not to be—but perhaps do not make pleasant hearing. Now, if the course of events will henceforth pass over the

[61] *Trierarchos*: performer of the liturgy of the *trierarchia*, involving maintaining for a year the hull, mast and sails of a trireme supplied by the State, furnishing the rest of the equipment, recruiting and training the crew and, finally, in the fifth century though not so often in the fourth, commanding the ship (hence: 'trierarch' or 'trireme-commander'). The cost of a trierarchy was nearly 1 talent (Lys. XXI.2), which cost was shared, after 358, by *symmoriai* (navy-boards), or groups of 60. Later the cost was subdivided even further; Jones, pp. 32-3. Cf. II.29 and note.
[62] If a man suspected that another was richer than he and should thus provide the liturgy in his place he could challenge him to take it over. If the other refused, the first could propose to exchange property with him. The case could then be referred to the generals for adjudication; Speech XLII deals with a case of this sort.
[63] Metics (*metoikoi*): 'resident aliens'; they were eligible for military service and paid normal taxes as well as a special annual tax but were not allowed to own land and had no political rights, except indirectly, through a patron or referee. This did not prevent their playing an important part in Athenian life; for example, Aristotle, Protagoras, Lysias and perhaps Aristophanes were metics. 'Dwellers apart' may mean either foreign-born residents who were not yet of metic status or freedmen; cf. *OCD* under 'Metic'. Harpocration explains the phrase as freedmen living apart from their old masters; or they may have been slaves established by their masters as independent workers on condition of the masters' receiving an agreed payment from the proceeds. Cf. *A Companion to Greek Studies*[4], p. 512.
[64] Cf. Dem. III.4-5 (with notes), which seems to provide a good example.
[65] Not published with the speech. The tactical advantages in controlling Euboea are obvious enough (cf. note 56, above). Athenians for this reason were

things that a speaker, so as to avoid giving offence, passes over in his speech, then one ought to speak only with a view to pleasing his audience. But if the charm of speeches, when it is not appropriate, results in reality in our personal damage, then it is shameful to deceive ourselves §39 and by putting off whatever is unpleasant always to be behind the action, unable to recognize even this fact, that those who engage correctly in warfare should not follow the course of events but should themselves be ahead of events; and that the policy-makers should be in command of events, exactly as one would expect a general to be in command of his forces, in order that whatever decisions they make may be executed and they may not be compelled to chase after the outcome of events. §40 But you, men of Athens, who possess the largest military resources of all—triremes, hoplites, cavalry and revenues[66]—you have never, up till this day, used any one of them as you ought; instead you wage war against Philip exactly in the way that barbarians box. For when one of these is hit he always clutches the place where the blow fell; and if you strike him in another place his hands move there. He neither knows how nor is willing to put up a defence or to stand up squarely to you. §41 And so with you. If you learn that Philip is in the Chersonese you vote to send an expedition there; if at Thermopylae, to there.[67] In fact you rush up and down after him, wherever he is, letting him act as your general. You yourselves have taken no useful decision about the war; before the event you see nothing until you hear that something either has happened or is happening. You may have been able to act thus in the past, but now the actual crisis has been reached and it is no longer possible.

§42 It seems to me, men of Athens, that some god, ashamed on the city's behalf at what is being done, has inspired Philip with this meddle-

---

conscious of its importance, to the extent that they were prepared to divide their forces by intervening there in 349/8 (cf. Cawkwell, *CQ* 1962, 127-30, and refs cited there).

[66] It is difficult to know how carefully D. is speaking here, whether his claim is any more than an exaggeration to stir Athenian pride. Only 3 years before, he admitted that the Persian king had greater resources in money and ships than Athens (XIV.9). After Athenian expenditure in and loss of allies after the Social War, the immediate need was felt to be financial recuperation—this indeed was the policy of Eubulus (*CAH* VI, 221-3; Cawkwell, *JHS* 1963, 43ff.). How far the situation may have improved in this short time is difficult to say, but in 352 (XXIII.209) D. spoke of the Treasury's containing barely provision for a day's march.

[67] By 'Chersonese', D. presumably means Heraion Teichos (§17 and notes), which is in fact in eastern Thrace. There is no evidence that Philip has been in the Chersonese by 350. However, Heraion Teichos might fairly be regarded by Athenians as a step in that direction (but §17: '. . . towards . . . the Chersonese . . .', is more accurate). For Thermopylae, §17 and notes, and Parke, p. 146.

Translation and Commentary: Philippic I

some activity of his. For if Philip, holding the places he has already subdued and seized, were willing to keep quiet and do no more, I think that some of you would be quite satisfied with a situation whereby we would stand convicted, as a people, of shameful conduct, of cowardice, of all that is most disgraceful.[68] But as it is, by always making new attempts and always striving for more, he might perhaps stir you to action, if you have not completely given up the struggle. §43 For my part, I am amazed that none of you either takes it to heart or is filled with indignation when he sees that although the war was begun with the object of punishing Philip[69] its end is already concerned with avoiding harm at Philip's hands. And yet it is quite obvious that he will not halt his progress unless he is compelled. Shall we wait for this? Do you think that all is well if you dispatch empty triremes[70] and send off the mere expectations that are being raised by so-and-so?[71] §44 Shall we not embark in our ships? Shall we not set out ourselves with at least part of our own citizen-forces now,[72] even if we have not done so before? Shall we not sail against Philip's territory?[73] But where, somebody asks me, shall we anchor off his coast? The war itself, men of Athens, will discover the weak point in his dispositions, if we make the attempt. But if we sit idly at home listening to the politicians abusing and blaming each other then certainly nothing will ever be done that should be done. §45 For in my opinion, wheresoever any part of our city—even if not the whole—is dispatched in company with the forces there fights along with it the good will of Heaven and of Fortune. But whenever you send out a commander, an empty decree and expressions of hope from the speaker's platform[74] none of the things are done that should be; instead, our enemies laugh at us while our allies stand in mortal fear of such expeditions. §46 For it is not possible, no, quite impossible that one single man could ever achieve for you all that you want achieved. He can, however, make promises, say 'yes' and accuse this man and that man; and the result of this is the ruin of our interests.[75] For when the

[68] Cf. III.8-9 and note.
[69] For the 'cause' of the war, Philip's action in taking Amphipolis (which he left autonomous) and Pydna in 357, cf. DS XVI.8.2-4, Dem. II.6-7, but also de Ste Croix, CQ 1963, 110-19.
[70] §19 and note.
[71] Cf. §45 below.
[72] Cf. §§21, 24-25.
[73] This is the only reference at all explicit to the proposed seat of operations. Cf. §50 and note.
[74] Cf. §§19, 24 and 43.
[75] There may, as some editors think, be an allusion here to the 'promises of Chares', proverbial for their unreliability. See also Dem. XXIII.154 for a similar indictment of Charidemus. So far as recriminations are concerned, an example D. probably has in mind is that of Chares, with his treatment of Iphicrates and Timotheus before Byzantium in 355 (DS XVI.21.1-4).

The Spectre of Philip

commander leads miserable, unpaid mercenaries, and when there are men here who glibly give you false information on his activities,[76] and when, on the basis of the stories you hear, you pass any decrees that come into your heads, then what must we expect?

§47 How, then, will this situation be ended?[77] It will cease when you, men of Athens, appoint the same men as soldiers and as witnesses of what the generals do, and as judges, when they have returned home, of the generals' auditing; in this way you will not only hear about your own affairs but will also be present and see them. As things are, our affairs have reached such a shameful state that each of the commanders is put on trial for his life twice or thrice in your courts,[78] but none of them dares engage in a struggle for life with your enemies even once;[79] they prefer to die the death of a kidnapper or a highwayman rather than the death appropriate to a soldier. For a criminal should die as the result of a court's sentence, a general fighting the enemy. §48 Some of us go about saying that Philip is planning with Sparta the destruction of Thebes and the dissolution of the democratic states, others that he has sent envoys to the Persian king, and still others that he is fortifying cities in Illyria—each one of us goes around inventing his own story.[80]

§49 For my part, men of Athens, I definitely think that Philip is intoxicated with the magnitude of his achievements and has many similar aspirations revolving in his mind; for he sees that there is nobody to stop him and he is buoyed up with his successes. I do not think, however, that he has chosen to act in such a way that the most foolish of our citizens know what he intends to do—for the rumourmongers are the most foolish of our citizens.[81]

§50 But if we give these tales short shrift and recognize that the fellow is an enemy, that he is depriving us of our possessions, that he has been wantonly outraging and insulting us for a long time, that all we ever expected anyone to do on our behalf has turned out to our detriment, that the future is in our own hands, that if we are not

[76] This refers to the practice of 'auditing' generals' behaviour with their armies before a jury of citizens, on the weakness of which cf. §47 and II.30.

[77] That is, the situation where a general in command of a mercenary force is recalled to Athens for trial by a citizen-jury, few if any of whom would have been eye-witnesses of his actions.

[78] Cf. DS XVI.21.1-4, Nepos *Chabrias* III.3, *Timotheus* III.4-5, *Iphicrates* III.3, Isoc. *Antidosis* 129, and Dinarchus I.14.

[79] An overstated and grossly unfair judgement on Athenian generals. See refs in note 78, above; also §§24, 19, 27 with notes, for the difficulties under which they often worked.

[80] We have no evidence to suggest that the stories are any more reliable than D. implies.

[81] §§48-49. In other words, let us act promptly on our information, but not on mere rumour.

Translation and Commentary: Philippic I

willing to fight Philip there[82] we may perhaps be forced to fight him here—if, I say, we recognize these things then we shall have made the necessary decision and have done with useless talk. For you must not inquire what the future will be; you must fully recognize that it will be bad if you do not give it your attention and are not willing to act appropriately.[83]

§51 I have never chosen on other occasions to speak with a view to pleasing you unless I was fully convinced it would be of benefit, and I have now given you my opinion freely and straightforwardly, with no reservations. I could wish that, just as I know it is beneficial for you to hear the best advice, so I knew that it would also be beneficial to the men who gave it; then I should be much happier. As it is, although it is not clear what will befall me as a result of this advice, I offer it nevertheless, convinced that it is to your benefit if you heed it.[84] May that prevail which is going to be to the advantage of all!

---

[82] Where? Perhaps in Macedonia (§44)? Does he anticipate facing Philip on his home ground with the force he has described? Philip is reputed to have used 30,000 men in his attacks on Perinthus and Byzantium in 340 (DS XVI.74.5).
[83] Cf. III.8-9 and note.
[84] Cf. §§38-39, III.21-22.

THE *OLYNTHIACS*

Speeches II, I, and III

PREFACE TO THE *OLYNTHIACS*

During the eighteen months between the end of 351 and mid-349, Philip seems to have remained quiet; at least, we have no record of his activities that can be dated with any confidence to that period. It remains for us, then, in this introduction, to examine the possible causes of his attack on the Chalcidian peninsula in 349/8.

Since 352, or earlier, the Olynthians had shown signs of dissatisfaction with their alliance with Philip. Overtures of peace had been made to Athens, with a promise of alliance to follow,[1] and although Philip had issued a severe caution, apparently accompanied by more active measures,[2] the pro-Athenian 'party' in Olynthus[3] apparently suffered no loss of prestige.

Why then did Olynthus turn against Philip? In the first place, this change of opinion, so blatantly overstated by Demosthenes, ought to be considered as a shift in relative popularity of the pro-Athenian and pro-Macedonian 'parties' respectively.[4] But this is no answer; a party's strength waxes or wanes generally according to public opinion. And we are reduced to guessing at the cause of this swing of opinion. Demosthenes' speech *Against Aristocrates* was delivered, so it is generally accepted, in the first-half of 352[5] and the new Olynthian development is reported for the first time in the course of it.[6] Cloché[7] suggests that Philip's conquest of Methone in 354, or his defeat of the Phocian army under Onomarchus or of the Thessalian tyrants at Pherae (which Cloché dates to 353, but both of which belong to 352)[8] might provide the motivation for Chalcidian fear of Philip.

These are all possibilities, depending on the exact date of the speech,

[1] XXIII.108-109, III.7 and note.
[2] IV.17, I.13 and note.
[3] II.1 and note.
[4] Ibid.
[5] Blass III.1.292.
[6] XXIII.108-109.
[7] Pp. 115-16.
[8] Cf. most lately, Ehrhardt, *CQ* 1967.

Preface to the Olynthiacs

but we can do more than guess. We may look further back, however, and question the Chalcidian motives in first agreeing to the alliance with Macedon in winter 357/6. By that time Athens had been embroiled in the struggle against her revolted allies, when they had to make a choice between the offers of alliance by Philip on the one hand and Athens on the other,[9] were undoubtedly forced to accept that of Philip, the close neighbour who was able to attack them long before they could expect effective help—indeed any help—from Athens. Thus, the Macedonian/Chalcidian alliance is no sure indication that the latter were *ever* favourably disposed towards Philip; their fear of him probably dates from the renaissance of Macedonian power in 359/8, though they felt unable to act until Athens had recovered somewhat from her defeat in the Social War (IV.40 and note). It ought also to be noted that the Olynthians, whatever they thought of Philip, certainly had no reason to love Athens (Marshall, pp. 93-5 with notes).

At any rate, in spite of Philip's severe warning at the end of 351, the Olynthians evidently persevered with their friendly overtures to Athens,[10] forcing Philip to take action. The alternative, his most dangerous enemy in league with his close neighbour, was unthinkable. He thus began an attack on the Chalcidian peninsula, city by city, which lasted about a year, culminating in the conquest of Olynthus in September 348.[11]

At an early stage of the Chalcidian campaign (probably about September 349) Philip's troubles were compounded by growing unrest in Thessaly,[12] which, however, he seems to have settled without much difficulty—apparently before the delivery of *Olynthiac* III, which does not mention it.

Again during the campaign, Athenian strength was divided by the dispatch of an expedition under Phocion to Euboea, at the request of Plutarchus of Eretria.[13] According to Plutarch[14] the trouble in Euboea

---

[9] DS XVI.8.3-5. Olynthus (as Chalcidians of Thrace) has been a member of the Second Athenian League but had defected in c. 369 with the renewal of Athenian attempts to take Amphipolis. Diodorus is not clear as to whether Athens was actually *offering* alliance (cf. Dem. II.6, which may represent only private initiative). At any rate, although the two possibilities were theoretically open to Olynthus, Athens was effectively ruled out by her preoccupation with the Social War.

[10] III.7 and notes. Cf. also Just. VIII.3.10 for what was perhaps the pretext for his attack.

[11] DS XVI.55, Dem. XIX.192. Note that the attack on Olynthus itself did not start before about May 348; it had not started when the second Athenian expedition arrived (Cawkwell, CQ 1962, 132).

[12] II.11, I.22; Sordi, pp. 263-5.

[13] Cf. V.5 and note for refs.

[14] *Phocion* 12-14.

was stirred up by Philip in order to distract Athens, but this view has been effectively challenged.[15] The campaign lasted only a month, from about mid-February to about mid-March, and was singularly unsuccessful. Demosthenes opposed the expedition, and was later proud of the fact.[16]

It was during the preparations for the Euboean expedition that Apollodorus proposed that the Theoric Fund be used for military purposes. Although he was successful, in that all the people supported him (or so the speaker of Dem.LIX would have it; §5), he was indicted for illegality and fined 15 talents, a very large amount.[17]

THE SPEECHES AND ATHENIAN AID TO OLYNTHUS

All three *Olynthiacs* were delivered early in 349/8, presumably shortly after the first appeal from Olynthus, which was issued undoubtedly as soon as the attacks began, or even earlier. At the time of this appeal, there was as yet no alliance; this was formed between the delivery of the first two and the third speeches.[18]

All three speeches were delivered before the dispatch of the first expedition, which was itself sent shortly after the forming of the alliance.[19] It seems likely, therefore, that they were delivered in fairly close succession,[20] perhaps, in one, two or all three cases, at special assembly meetings, rather than at three consecutive, ordinary meetings in three successive prytanies.[21]

The expeditions, described by Philochorus,[22] were as follows. The first, commanded by Chares, comprised 2,000 peltast mercenaries and 30 triremes, as well as 8 others, manned by Athenians for the occasion; the second, under Charidemus, who was the current commander at the Hellespont, 4,000 peltast mercenaries, 150 cavalry and 18 triremes; the third, again under Chares, 2,000 Athenian hoplites, 300 cavalry in horse-transports and '17 other triremes'. Cawkwell[23] concludes that the first

[15] Cawkwell, *CQ* 1962, 129-30.
[16] V.5.
[17] Cf. my Appendix, *The Theorikon*.
[18] A comparison of II.2, I.2,10 with III.7-8 would suggest this. Also note the changed attitude of Demosthenes towards Olynthus in Speech III; cf. II.23 and note.
[19] Philochorus F 49 (through D.Hal. *ep. ad Amm.* I.9, *ll.* 5-12); Cawkwell, *CQ* 1962, 130 n. 7; Croiset, *Harangues*, pp. 90-1.
[20] Although this cannot be taken to the extreme of Erbse's suggestion, *RhM* 1956, 364-80, that all three speeches were spoken on the same day; for contrary indications, cf. notes to I.22, II.23, III.8.
[21] It does not seem possible to fit the two and a half months necessary for this arrangement into the time before the first expedition, if Philochorus' implication (my note 19 above) is correctly interpreted.
[22] Ff. 49-51 (D.Hal. *ep. ad Amm.* I.9).
[23] *CQ* 1962, 131.

expedition, apart from the extra 8 triremes,[24] was merely the permanent force stationed at the Hellespont. Also, he suggests that Charidemus' 18 triremes, in the second expedition, might have been the 8 manned by Athenian volunteers, added to the 10 with which he left Athens in September 351. Of the third expedition, Philochorus specifies '17 *other* triremes', implying, Cawkwell conjectures, that they were the only ships apart from—or including?—the 8 mentioned above specially sent out from Athens during the whole war. As Chares is then cited as leader of 'the whole force', the implication is that these 17 were added to the force already there. That is, there were, presumably, 30 plus 18 (or only 10, or only 8?) plus 17 triremes in the third expedition—which arrived after Olynthus had fallen. Obviously, Athens sent very little special help, and, even though the third expedition may have been delayed by the Etesian winds, the larger part of the force must have been in the north already.[25]

A comparison of the enthusiastic action urged by Demosthenes in the *Olynthiacs* with the strength of the forces actually sent indicates strongly that the orator did not receive a sympathetic hearing.[26] In fact, it is quite clear that *in 349/8, Demosthenes' fears of Philip were not those of the majority of the Athenian population*, and we shall misinterpret the whole situation if we imagine they were.[27]

THE ORDER OF THE *Olynthiacs*[28]

As I have shown elsewhere,[29] it is my opinion that the order in which the *Olynthiacs* were delivered is II-I-III, that proposed by Stueve and Grote in the nineteenth century.[30]

---

[24] Cf. Dem. XXI.161.

[25] Demosthenes' later estimate, XIX.266, of 10,000 mercenaries, 50 triremes and 4,000 citizens, obviously does not square with these figures. However, the context of his estimate, in which he stresses the inadequacy of the most effective forces in the face of pro-Philip traitors, may suggest to us that we ought to be wary of attaching much credence to it; the more he exaggerates the figures, the more striking his point becomes. Cf. Beloch III.1.496; Parke, p. 148.

[26] Cf. Libanius' Introduction to *Olynthiac* II with note.

[27] Thus, while Jaeger, p. 125, concedes that political speeches and facts are two very different quantities, he is so convinced by Demosthenes' words that he says, only two pages below (p. 127), that 'even the members of the peace party in Athens proposed immediate action in support of Olynthus', which was patently not so.

[28] For a history of the dispute on the order, cf. Grote, Vol. XI (1869 edn), his Appendix 'On the Order of the Olynthiac Orations of Demosthenes', pp. 163-7. For a more detailed presentation of the arguments below *see* Ellis, *Historia* 1966, 297-301. Cf. also III.8-9 and note.

[29] III.8-9 and note.

[30] Grote, Vol. XI, ibid.

The Spectre of Philip

Two considerations led to this conclusion, the first inconclusive, the second rather more definite. First, it is strange that in Speech I Demosthenes mentioned the Theoric Fund (§19), whereas he ignored it completely in Speech II, before attacking it directly in III (§§10-13). The II-I-III order allows for the increasing urgency of the situation—in Demosthenes' eyes, at any rate—to show through the orator's increasing willingness to risk unpopularity by suggesting reform of the laws.[31]

Second, there is the change in the Thessalian situation shown in II.11 and I.22. II.11 makes it apparent that the Thessalians have just voted to demand back Pagasae and to discuss the question of Philip's continuing occupation of Magnesia, whereas, in I.22, it is stated that (a) 'they have voted to demand Pagasae back from him' and (b) *'have stopped him fortifying* Magnesia' and further, be it at this stage only a rumour,[32] (c) will 'no longer grant him the enjoyment of the revenues of their harbours and markets'. There can be little doubt, unless the text is to be distorted, that this order—II.11 followed by I.22—is the natural one.

Thus we have arranged the *Olynthiacs* in this revised order, II-I-III, which involves one difficulty. Libanius believed the speeches to have been delivered in the conventional order and consequently wrote the long general Introduction to accompany Speech I, with only a short connecting Introduction to II (as with III). Rather than attaching each to its correct speech and thus putting the Introductions in an order other than that intended for them, we have placed them together in the order I-II-III before the speeches in the revised order.

---

[31] Cf. my Appendix, *The Theorikon*.
[32] Which was presumably based on fact, if Philip was moved to intervene while in the middle of his Chalcidian campaign; Sordi, pp. 263-5.

LIBANIUS' INTRODUCTION TO SPEECH I

§1 Olynthus was a city in Thrace. The people who inhabited this area[1] were by race Greek, from Chalcis in Euboea.[2] Chalcis was an Athenian colony. Olynthus had many glorious wars to its credit. They waged war against the Athenians, when in older times the latter were ruling the Greeks, and again against the Spartans.[3] In time the city attained great power and held sway over its sister-cities[4] (for Thrace was well populated with people of Chalcidian origin). §2 The Olynthians made an alliance with Philip, king of Macedonia,[5] and waged war along with him, at first against the Athenians. From the Macedonians they received Anthemus,[6] a city that was disputed by the Macedonians and the Olynthians; then they received Potidaea,[7] which was disputed by the Athenians, but was taken after a siege by Philip and handed over to the Olynthians. Later, however, they began to view the king with suspicion,[8] for they saw that the increase of his power had been swift and extensive and that his intentions were not to be trusted. They waited till he was away from Macedonia then sent an embassy to the Athenians and made a settlement to the war between them.[9] This they did in contravention of the treaty

---

[1] The Chalcidians; Strabo VII.10.68, F 11; Hdt. VIII.127.
[2] For a short study of the early inhabitants of Chalcidice see Gude, pp. 1-6.
[3] Olynthus, a member of the Delian League (Thuc. V.18.5), revolted in 432, along with other Chalcidians and the Potidaeans, at the instigation of Perdiccas II of Macedon (Thuc. I.56-65). The rebellion continued until 421, when Chalcidice entered into alliance with Corinth (Thuc. V.30-31, 38). It seems probable that the Chalcidians were neutral for the last 10 years of the Peloponnesian War (Gude, p. 17). Later they were members of the anti-Spartan coalition in the Corinthian War (DS XIV.82). At some time between 389 and 383, Amyntas III of Macedon formed a defensive alliance 'for 50 years' with them (Tod No. 111), but by 383 he was their enemy (DS XV.19.2-3). Xen. HG V.2.11-3.26 recounts the battles of 383-379 between Sparta and Olynthus that resulted in a negotiated peace (cf. Dem. XIX.264 on the peace).
[4] For the formation of the Chalcidian League, a much-debated question see Gude, pp. 18-23.
[5] Olynthian/Macedonian alliance, winter 357/6; Dem. XXIII.108, II.14, VI.20.
[6] Dem. VI.20; apparently just before the alliance. Anthemus is a district not a city.
[7] Plut. Al. III, Just. XII.16. This was a few months after the treaty; II.7 and notes.
[8] Dem. XXIII.108-109.
[9] Ibid.

The Spectre of Philip

with Philip, for they had agreed together to wage war jointly against the Athenians and, should a different policy be decided upon, to make peace jointly. §3 Now Philip had long been looking for an excuse against the Olynthians and, having obtained this excuse, he made war upon them on the grounds that they had violated the treaty and had made a pact of friendship with his enemies.[10] The situation then is that the Olynthians have sent an embassy to Athens for assistance,[11] and Demosthenes is supporting their pleas, bidding his countrymen to send aid to Olynthus.[12] He says that the preservation of Olynthus means the safety of Athens. For, he says, if the Olynthians are preserved, Philip will never march against Attica[13] and Athens will be able to sail against Macedonia and conduct the war there.[14] But, he maintains, if Olynthus should be subdued by Philip, the road to Athens will have been opened to the king. And he says that Philip is not as hard to fight as has popularly been believed;[15] in this way he tries to embolden the Athenians against him.

§4 He has also discussed the public finances, advising the Athenians to make them available for military instead of theoric purposes.[16] This custom that the Athenians followed is not easily understood and I must explain it. In olden days in Athens there was no stone theatre, only wooden benches that were fitted together.[17] Everybody used to scramble for a seat and there used to be blows and even injuries. The Athenian government wanted to prevent this, so they made the seats subject to purchase. Each person had to give 2 obols and, having paid the price, could watch the performance. So that the poor might not appear to be burdened by the expense it was ordained[18] that each person should

---

[10] Libanius is compressing the events of several years into one (cf. the Preface to the *Olynthiacs*, Speeches II, I, and III, and my Appendix, 'Chronological Table'). Philip *had* an excuse in 352 and 351 (Dem. XXIII.108-109) but did not take advantage of it. What prompted him to begin the war in 349 we can only conjecture; cf. Preface to the *Olynthiacs*, III.7 and notes, I.3-4; also Just. VIII.3.10.

[11] Philochorus F 49 (our Appendix, 'Selection of Historical Fragments'), Plut. *Mor.* 845D; probably in September or October 349, immediately after the outbreak of the war.

[12] §§2-5, 6-7, 17-18, 25-28.

[13] §§12-13, 14-15, 25-28.

[14] §28.

[15] §§21-24; cf. also II.5-10, 14-21.

[16] §§19-20; cf. also III.10-13, 19-20, 33-34.

[17] The benches were assembled probably only for performances. Evidence on the fifth-century Athenian theatre is meagre; cf. Robertson, *Greek and Roman Architecture*, p. 164.

[18] By Pericles(?); Plut. *Peric.* IX; Philochorus F 33, and our Appendix, 'Selection of Historical Fragments'; but compare Just. VI.9.2; Cawkwell, *JHS* 1963, 55 n. 53. Also cf. §20 below, Schwahn in *RE* under 'Theorikon'; Isoc. *On the Peace* 82.

Libanius' Introduction to Speech I

receive his 2 obols from the Treasury. This then was the origin of the custom, and it reached such a pitch that they not only received money for the theatre-seats, but simply divided among themselves all the public revenues.[19] §5 The result was that they were also made hesitant about going on campaign. For of old the citizens used to receive pay from the State when they went on campaign, but now they remained at home amidst theatre-shows and festivals, and divided the money amongst themselves. Therefore they were no longer willing to go out and face dangers, and they passed a law concerning these theoric monies, threatening capital punishment to anyone who proposed that they should be transferred back to their former arrangement and become military funds. This is why Demosthenes treads so carefully in his advice concerning this matter, and, after asking himself the question 'Are you proposing that these monies should be used for military purposes?', gives the answer 'Good lord, not I!'[20] So much then for the Theoric Fund.[21]

§6 The orator has also discussed a citizen-force, claiming that the Athenians should serve in person on campaign and should not render their assistance, as they were accustomed, by means of mercenaries.[22] For, he says, this is the reason why our affairs are going to rack and ruin.

---

[19] A gross misinterpretation; cf. my Appendix, *The Theorikon*.
[20] §19.
[21] For a discussion of the Theoric Fund *see* my Appendix, *The Theorikon*.
[22] §6; cf. also II.27, III.35, IV.19, 24, 46.

LIBANIUS' INTRODUCTION TO SPEECH II

The Athenians admitted the embassy of the Olynthians and have decided to help them. But they are hesitating over actually marching out to war and are in a state of fear, thinking that waging war on Philip is no easy matter. Demosthenes therefore comes to the rostrum and attempts to encourage the people by pointing out that the Macedonian's affairs are shaky. For, he says, Philip is viewed with suspicion by his allies and he is not strong in his own national forces, because the Macedonians by themselves are weak.[1]

---

[1] Libanius has events confused, due partly to his ordering of the *Olynthiacs* in the now-traditional manner (I-II-III) and partly to his unstated assumption that each of D.'s speeches on Olynthus must have resulted in some action. (This latter is probably based on an earlier misconception, that D. by 349 had already reached a position of influence in Athens, whereas there is no evidence for his ascendancy until 343, when, in spite of a complete lack of genuine evidence against Aeschines, he failed only by the narrowest of margins to convict him of improper behaviour on the second embassy of 346.) Thus he assumes that *Olynthiac* I produced the agreement to the Olynthian alliance, *Olynthiac* II the second expedition and *Olynthiac* III the subsequent two expeditions. Modern studies, on the contrary, have indicated that all three speeches precede the first expedition; cf. Preface to the *Olynthiacs*.

LIBANIUS' INTRODUCTION TO SPEECH III

The Athenians sent aid to the Olynthians and appeared to be gaining some success by it—and they were kept informed of this. The people are overjoyed and the politicians are encouraging them to take vengeance on Philip. Demosthenes, therefore, is afraid that the people may become over-confident, believing that they have carried all before them and have sent sufficient aid to Olynthus, thus neglecting all that still remains to be done.[1] For this reason, when he has come forward to speak, he rebukes their boastfulness and tries to turn their minds to a prudent caution, saying that their present debate is not concerned with exacting vengeance on Philip but with the safety of their allies. For he knows that the Athenians and certain other peoples, although taking care not to neglect their own possessions, are less zealous when it comes to punishing their enemies. In this speech he also touches more openly on advice concerning the theoric monies,[2] and he asks for the repeal of the laws that impose a penalty on those who propose that they become military monies, in order that there may be no fear attached to giving the best counsel. He also advises them generally to rouse themselves to an emulation of their ancestors and to serve on campaign in person.[3] And he engages in considerable censure against both the people, as being dissolute, and the popular leaders, as not giving a proper lead to the city.[4]

---

[1] Libanius is reading far too much into the tone of the proem (§§1-3). Certainly no aid has yet been sent to Olynthus (Olynthus itself has not yet been attacked; cf. my Appendix, 'Chronological Table').
[2] §§10-13, 19-20, 33-34; cf. my Appendix, *The Theorikon*. D. does not ask that the laws imposing a penalty on those attempting to alter the theoric laws be repealed; he asks that the theoric laws themselves be revoked. There was no special penalty involved until after Apollodorus' attempt in 349. D.'s fear was of the *graphe paranomon*, the normal restriction on unconstitutional proposals (cf. ibid.).
[3] §§21-28.
[4] §§29-36.

TRANSLATION AND COMMENTARY
Olynthiac II—August/September(?) 349

§1 On many occasions, men of Athens, it seems to me, one can see the good will of Heaven openly manifesting itself to our city, but especially in the present situation. For it certainly seems like a divinely inspired blessing that there have arisen men[1] to fight Philip, men who possess territory bordering on his and who have some military resources,[2] men —and this is the most important point—whose attitude towards the war is such that they believe that a reconciliation with Philip is both untrustworthy and tantamount to the destruction of their own country.[3]
§2 Therefore, men of Athens, it is up to us now to see to it that we do not appear less concerned for ourselves than circumstances are for us. For to be seen throwing to the four winds not only the cities and regions we once controlled but also the allies and the opportunities provided for us by Fortune is the sign of men of little honour, or rather of no honour at all.[4]

§3 I do not think, men of Athens, that it is a good thing to give a

---

[1] I.e., the Olynthians.
[2] According to D.'s later estimate (XIX.263-266) their (military?) strength at this time was over 10,000 infantry with 1,000 cavalry (compared with 400 cavalry and a grand total of 5,000 in about 380). The figure for 349/8 may be exaggerated, as the orator's intention is to stress the impotence of large native and relief-forces in the face of the treachery of the pro-Macedonian party in Olynthus (on which, Xen. *HG* V.2.11ff., which shows the strong motivation for such a party). In any case, part at least of the increase is due to the inclusion of the other Chalcidian forces (XIX.263-266).
[3] Cf. I.5; also IX.11. Whatever he intends people to think, D. is not speaking here for the whole Olynthian population. There is a pro-Macedonian party that has hitherto, apparently, been in the majority, but is now overshadowed by a pro-Athenian group. One of the major problems for Athens, in making a decision to help is this: should the pro-Macedonian regain the ascendancy, any Athenian relief-force might well find itself opposed to the combined forces of Macedonia and Olynthus. In fact, the city was 'betrayed' by the pro-Macedonian group (VIII.40, XIX.265, 342). While D. was not to know this would happen, he ought to have considered it as a possibility before proposing to send Athenian help. Had the third expedition arrived before (instead of after) the fall of the city, it might have suffered the same fate as the pro-Athenian Olynthians.
[4] Cf. III.8-9 and notes.

description of Philip's strength and by means of such an account to try to encourage you to do your duty. For it seems to me that anything anybody could say on this subject only brings glory to Philip and displays our own failures. For the more that Philip has attained success beyond his deserts, the greater is the admiration with which everyone regards him; but with you, the more you have failed to make fitting use of your opportunities, the greater is the disgrace you have incurred.[5] Therefore I shall pass over these matters.[6] §4 In fact, men of Athens, if one were to examine the matter honestly, he would see that Philip's rise to greatness derives from here,[7] not from his own efforts. However, I do not consider this to be the proper time to talk about the debts that Philip owes to our politicians who act on his behalf or about the punishment you ought to impose on them. What I shall attempt to tell you are the matters outside this subject which can be dealt with, matters you all ought to hear of, and which if you examine them correctly, will appear as sources of reproach against Philip.

§5 Now one might say—and with justice—that to call Philip a breaker of his sworn oath and a faithless fellow, without showing what he has done, is merely to indulge in empty abuse. However, it so happens that it needs only a few words to recount all he has ever done up to now and to prove him guilty on every occasion. And I think that these words ought to be spoken, for two reasons: firstly, so that it may be obvious that Philip is a paltry foe (and this really is the case);[8] secondly, so that those who stand aghast before him, as though he were some invincible being, may see that he has now exhausted all the means of deceit whereby in the past he has risen to greatness, and that his career of success has now reached its very limit.

§6 For my part, men of Athens, I too would consider Philip a very terrible and amazing man if I saw that he had attained prominence by pursuing a policy of justice. But as it is, as I examine his career, I find that, by saying he would hand over Amphipolis[9] and by fabricating that

---

[5] Cf. IV.6-7.

[6] D. does not act upon these words elsewhere (e.g., I.8-9, 12-13); it is a mere rhetorical point. It does however suggest that this speech was not delivered on the same day as *Olynthiac* I (as Erbse, *RhM* 1956, 364-80), as the inconsistency would have been all too plain.

[7] 'Here', meaning either 'Athens' or perhaps 'this very rostrum' (from which orators addressed the assembly on the Pnyx; for the Pnyx cf. Kourounitios and Thompson, *Hesperia* 1932, 90).

[8] If D. really believes this he has a very poor comprehension of Philip's ability and resources (but cf. IV.4, where he contradicts himself). This is merely cheap encouragement; strangely so, because he is urging expensive forces to fight Philip (I.17-18).

[9] Cf. VII.27, DS XVI.8, Theopompus F 30 (our Appendix, 'Selection of Historical Fragments') H&H No. 125. Dated variously between 359 and 357. Whether

'secret clause' that everyone talked about, he won over our simple souls right at the beginning,[10] when certain people were for expelling from Athens the Olynthians when they wished to hold discussions with you;[11] §7 that he then procured the friendship of the Olynthians by seizing Potidaea—which was your possession—and by wronging his former allies and handing them over to Olynthus;[12] and that now, finally, he has won over the Thessalians by promising to hand over Magnesia to them

---

Philip actually said this or expressed friendship in terms that Athens took to mean that he ceded all claims to Amphipolis or whether D. is inventing it we do not know. But it seems very strange for Philip to have so obviously provoked the enmity of Athens before she was involved in the Social War and before he had an alliance with Chalcidice. De Ste Croix (CQ 1963, 110-18) provides a very useful treatment of the question.

[10] The meaning of 'that notorious secret' is unknown (de Ste Croix, CQ 1963, esp. 118). It has usually been taken to refer to a secret agreement between Philip and Athens, whereby the former would cede Amphipolis to Athens in exchange for Pydna. However, constitutionally this was not practicable; moreover it would make nonsense of the sentence, which would then read '. . . by saying he would hand over Amphipolis and by "fabricating" that secret agreement to hand over Amphipolis in exchange for Pydna. . . .'

[11] 357? Possibly when Philip was menacing Amphipolis.

[12] All the translations of this speech show a different rendering of this claim. Thus, for example, the Loeb translation (*Demosthenes*, Vol. I, p. 27) runs: '. . . next [he won] the friendship of the Olynthians by capturing Potidaea, which was yours, and thus wronging you, his former allies, in presenting it to them'. Blass however deletes the 'you' (cf. *Demosthenes*, Vol. I, p. 27 n.b.), considering it a later gloss to explain 'the former allies' and de Ste Croix (CQ 1963, 111 n. 1) has supported this on historical grounds. This makes 'the former allies', as we have translated it here, the Potidaeans. Although it may seem strange for an Athenian cleruchy to have had the authority to make an alliance with another power, this is what D. means (cf. also VII.10). At some time during the years 359-357, then, the Potidaeans were in alliance with Philip. Potidaea had been a member of the Chalcidian League until forcibly detached by Timotheus in c. 364 (Isoc. *Antidosis* 108, 113; Dinarchus I.14; DS XVI.81.6). This separation was reinforced by a request in 361 for cleruchs, which Athens duly sent (Tod No. 146; Dem. VII.10). *See also* Pickard-Cambridge, *Public Orations* (Demosthenes), p. 100. If Potidaea was Philip's ally in the first 2 or 3 years of his reign, this agreement will certainly have been dissolved at the time of Athens' declaration of war in late 357. For this reason, and because Philip was naturally opposed to what was virtually an Athenian base near his own and on his ally's territory, it is hardly valid to imply, as D. does here, that Philip was breaking faith with his allies. Moreover, the impression given here—although probably not to D.'s audience—is that Philip held out Potidaea as a bribe to the Olynthians to gain their alliance (as he did with Anthemus; VI.20). But as he did not attack Potidaea (spring or early summer 356) for some months after the Macedonian/Chalcidian alliance was formed (winter, early 356; Beloch III.1.230), he could at the most have promised to hand it over if he were successful in taking it (cf. also VII.9, 10, 13, VIII.62, 65).

Translation and Commentary: Olynthiac II

and by undertaking to fight the Phocian war on their behalf.[13] In short there is no one who has had dealings with Philip whom he has not cheated. For his method of aggrandizement has always been to beguile and to win over, one after another, those whose folly prevented their seeing him as he is. §8 And so, just as Philip has attained greatness by these means, each state thinking that he would serve its own interests, so it is proper that he be pulled down again by these same means, now that he has been shown to do everything for his own gain.[14] This, men of Athens, is the crisis Philip's affairs have reached. If anyone disagrees, let him come forward now and show me—or rather, show you—either that what I say is not true or that men who have been deceived at the outset will ever again trust their deceiver or that men who have been reduced to slavery contrary to their deserts would not be glad to regain their liberty.[15]

§9 If any one of you thinks this is the case but believes that Philip will maintain his position by force because he has already seized the fortified positions, the harbours and suchlike, then he is wrong. For whenever a political association is formed on the basis of goodwill and when all who participate in a war have the same advantage to be gained from it, then men are willing to toil together, to bear misfortunes and to endure trouble. But whenever anyone, like Philip, has become strong as a result of grasping arrogance and wickedness, the first excuse and the first small mistake are enough to upset and disrupt his whole position.[16] §10 For it is not possible, men of Athens, for a wrongdoer, for a perjurer, for a liar to win power of an enduring nature; such things hold out for the moment and for a short while—indeed, it may be that they blossom brightly on the hopes they raise—but in time they are found out and

---

[13] As yet Philip has not been able to carry out these promises. He has so far intervened in the Sacred War against the Phocians and, thus, in the interests of the Thessalians (Westlake, Chapter 8; Sordi, Chapter 9), but he has not yet handed over Magnesia (cf. II.11, I.22, Isoc. *Philippus* 21, Dem. VI.22).

[14] This is a good example of a type of special pleading to which D., in common with politicians of all ages, is very prone (cf., e.g., §§3, 15, 22). While it is legitimate for Athens to act in her own interests, it is not legitimate, he is saying, when Philip acts in his. (This common logical fallacy is explained and usefully illustrated by Stebbing, *Thinking to Some Purpose*, Penguin, London 1948, Chapter 4, esp. pp. 52-4.) It can hardly be doubted that the primary task of any leader is to act in the genuine interest of his country, and it is clearly in the interest of Macedonia that alliances and buffer-states be formed to preserve her from the powers that have preyed on her in the past (cf. for example, H&H No. 95; Xen. *HG* V.2.12-13, 16; and Thuc. IV.108).

[15] Note the emotive use of 'slavery' and 'liberty'.

[16] D. continues the form of special pleading noted above (§8 and note). When he extols the virtues of Athenian imperialism in the past (e.g., II.21-27, esp. 26), he does not concede that the motives he commends are just those that he imputes to and condemns in Philip.

collapse about themselves. For I think that just as the foundations of a house, a ship and such things should be the strongest part, so too the principles and foundations of men's actions must be honest and just. And this is just not true of the things Philip has done.

§11 I say then that you must send help to Olynthus—and the best and speediest way that is proposed has my approval. To the Thessalians you must dispatch an embassy whose task will be to point out these facts to some states and to give encouragement to others[17]—for even now they have voted to demand back Pagasae and to hold discussions about Magnesia.[18] §12 But see to it, men of Athens, that our envoys do not only make speeches; let them have some solid action they can point to, when you have taken the field in a manner worthy of the city and are right on top of the course of events. For all talk without actions appears an empty and an idle thing—especially talk that comes from our city; for the more we appear to engage in talk with the utmost readiness, the more is it universally held in suspicion. §13 You must show them a deep change and a great alteration in your ways, by paying the war-tax, by taking the field[19] and by doing everything with a will, if anyone is to take notice of you. And if you are willing actually to perform all these things in the proper manner, not only will Philip's alliances be shown to be weak and unreliable, but also the parlous condition of his own empire and power will be made manifest.

§14 For in general the power and realm of Macedonia is not a negligible factor when it is added to another power, as you found it when it gave you help against Olynthus in Timotheus' time.[20] Again this is how it appeared to the Olynthians, when combined with their own forces, in their struggle with the Potidaeans.[21] And, most recently, it

[17] These 'facts' may be the 'facts' of Philip's potential and actual weakness (§§5-10; cf. Erbse, *RhM* 1956, 375-6), or they may be the news of Athens' impending action. The dissatisfaction of the Thessalians is mentioned in both of the first two *Olynthiacs* but not in the third, which suggests that Philip, in the interim, has intervened in some way, perhaps with further promises (Westlake, p. 184; Sordi, pp. 263-5, collects the evidence for an intervention of some kind).
[18] Cf. I.22. Note that here (II.11) the Thessalians have voted to demand back Pagasae and *to hold discussions about Magnesia* (§7 and note), whereas in I.22 they have voted to demand back Pagasae and *have hindered* the fortifying of Magnesia. Cf. Ellis, *Historia* 1966, 297-301.
[19] Cf. IV.7 and note.
[20] c. 364; cf. IV.27, Tod No. 143. This is probably a reference to the aid furnished to Timotheus by Menelaus the Lynkestian, or Pelagonian, for which he was thanked in a decree of 363/2. Some editors (e.g., Loeb, *Demosthenes*, Vol. I, p. 30) take this as a reference to an agreement between Timotheus and Perdiccas III of Macedon (365/4-360/59), at the beginning of the latter's reign (Polyaenus III.10, 14; Beloch III.1.195).
[21] The attack on Potidaea (early summer 356) was conducted some months after the formation of the Macedonian/Chalcidian alliance (winter 357/6). Cf. §7

aided the Thessalians in their dissensions and struggles against the family of the tyrants.[22] Indeed, in my opinion, the addition anywhere of even a small force benefits the whole. But by itself this power of Philip's is weak and riddled with defects. §15 For by all these things whereby one might think of him as being a strong man—his wars and his campaigns, I mean—Philip has in fact created for himself an even greater instability in his realm than it used naturally to possess. For do not suppose, men of Athens, that Philip and his subjects take delight in the same things. Philip desires glory and has made this his ambition; he has elected to act, to run risks, and while so doing to suffer any misfortunes that may arise, preferring the renown of achieving what no other Macedonian king has achieved to living a life of safety.[23] §16 His subjects, however, have no part in the glory that accrues from these actions; they are worn out and fed up with these campaigns of his here, there, and everywhere, and they endure unending hardships. For they are neither allowed to spend time on their jobs or their personal affairs nor can they dispose of whatever they produce, as best they are able, since all the trading marts in the land have been closed because of the war.[24]

§17 It is quite easy to learn from these factors how the majority of the Macedonians regard Philip. And what about foreigners[25] and Foot-

---

and note, and Beloch III.1.230. It appears that the Olynthians actually fought with Philip in the attack on Potidaea.

[22] The tyrants at Pherae, defeated in 352 by Philip and the Thessalian League (DS XVI.37.3; for the chronology Hammond, *JHS* 1937, 56-7, 66-8).

[23] D. cannot see or will not concede that no king of a united Macedonia can possibly live a 'life of safety' until the threats offered by Thrace, Chalcidice, and Athens are removed.

[24] This after 8 to 9 years of Philip's reign. Yet in the remaining 14 until his death, with one special exception (DS XVI.35.2), there is no indication that his army and his people were unwilling to follow him. We know nothing of his rates of pay for military service, in fact little enough of Alexander's (Berve I.193-5; in spite of attempts to prove otherwise), but we do know that at least the Companions and officers were given large tracts of land from conquered territories (Theopompus F 224-5; our Appendix, 'Selection of Historical Fragments' below; and Parke, p. 160), and this may well have applied on a smaller scale to all his national soldiers. While it may be true that some of the Macedonian markets or trade-lines—the Chalcidian ones—are closed, Macedonia is a far more self-sufficient country than Attica. Even ignoring possible trade with other northern countries (Thessaly, Thrace, Illyria, Paeonia, Epirus, etc.) Macedonia without Chalcidice is on a much sounder economic footing than Athens without the Hellespont. And with Byzantium and Perinthus for allies Philip might have seriously jeopardized the security of the Athenian corn-route. This appears to be false encouragement. Cf. §5 and note, above.

[25] *Xenoi*—'foreigners' may also mean 'mercenaries'. Philip certainly had mercenaries by this time; DS XVI.8.7; Parke, pp. 156-7, 161-2. But there are also many stories, some very probably apocryphal, attesting the presence of foreigners at

The Spectre of Philip

Companions[26] who cluster around him? They have a reputation for being supermen and for possessing superb discipline and *esprit de corps*, but they are no better than any other soldiers, as I heard from somebody who had actually been in Macedonia—a man totally incapable of lying. §18 He said that Philip's jealousy makes him reject any of his Companions who is experienced in war and battles;[27] for he wants it to appear that all achievements are his own. 'For', said my informant, 'in addition to his other faults, Philip's jealousy is insurpassable.' Furthermore, he said, if anyone there is sober-minded and just and cannot bear the daily incontinence of Philip's life, his drunkenness and wild dancing, such a man is pushed aside and held of no account. §19 All that are left, he continued, are bandits, flatterers and the sort of men who get themselves blind drunk and then indulge in such dances as I shrink from naming to you here. And it is obvious that these statements are true. For Philip welcomes and keeps at his court the men whom everyone was for expelling from Athens because they were much more outrageous

---

Philip's court. If Theopompus can be trusted in any judgement involving morals (Murray, pp. 162-4), Philip 'bought' the attendance of all manner of men, known for their ability in many fields (Theopompus F 81, 224, 225; our Appendix, 'Selection of Historical Fragments', also Athenaeus VI.248D, XIV.614DE; Dem. II.19). It does appear, once the bias is removed from these accounts, that Philip encouraged foreign talent. We should probably, then, read both 'foreigners' and 'mercenaries' in this context; cf. Parke, pp. 160-2.

[26] *Pezetairoi*: 'Foot-Companion' founded according to Anaximenes F 4 (our Appendix, 'Selection of Historical Fragments'), by Alexander (perhaps Alexander II, 370/69 BC, certainly not Alexander III, the Great). Distinct from the *hetairoi* ('Companion cavalry'), they were the national territorial levies of Macedonia; Tarn II.135-6, Berve I.112-13. This is the first known reference to *pezetairoi*. In general on the Macedonian army, Tarn II.135ff., Berve I.103ff.; Griffith, *PCPhS* 1956/7, 3-10; *G&R* 1965, 125ff.; and Milns, *Historia* 1967, 509-12.

[27] This imputation and those following in §§18-19 are fairly common in later writers on Philip and are derived from Theopompus and Demosthenes. D. of course had his reasons for this sort of attack; charges of (especially sexual) immorality are easy to make and more inflammatory than political or ethical arguments (cf. for example, J. Milton, *First Defence of the People of England*, 1652 (against Salamasius)). Theopompus' reason may be a little different. Although, as a Chian living in Athens, he probably had no love for Philip, his main motive in his attacks (as Murray says, pp. 149-70, esp. 162) is perhaps to be found in his Cynicism. At any rate we must treat such evidence with care because, especially in the present example, (a) in terms of rhetorical expediency, it suits D. well to invent it, or (b) it may simply be the result of exaggerated misunderstanding between cultures alien to each other in many respects. For similar references see §17 and note. In general we may note that accusations of this sort sit unhappily beside D.'s grudging admissions of Philip's efficiency (e.g., I.5, IV.41-42). Cf. also Plut. *Dem.* 20, Theopompus F 236, our Appendix, 'Selection of Historical Fragments', but compare Just. IX.4.1-3.

than professional conjurers; for example, the notorious public slave, Callias, and men like him, actors of farces and composers of rude verses, which they make up about their companions in order to get a laugh.[28] §20 You may think these are small things, men of Athens, but to intelligent people they are very good evidence of Philip's disposition and of the way he is possessed by the forces of evil. However, his success, I feel, now tends to obscure these facts (for successes have a marvellous ability to cover up such scandalous happenings as these). But if once he makes a mistake, then people will examine these qualities of his more closely. And I think, men of Athens, that it will not be long before they are brought into the open, if Heaven is willing and you wish it. §21 For, just as in the human body, as long as a person is in good health he feels nothing wrong with himself; but when some malady comes upon him, his whole system is disturbed, be the upset a rupture, a sprain or any other weakness in his constitution. So it is in the case of cities and of despots: as long as they wage war outside their own territories most people cannot see their weaknesses. But once they become entangled in a war on their own borders, it brings out everything into the open.

§22 If any one of you, men of Athens, as he looks on Philip's good fortune, thinks that this makes Philip a formidable opponent to fight against, his reasoning is that of an intelligent person. For good luck carries great weight—rather it means everything—throughout all human affairs. I personally, however, were I given the choice, would choose the good fortune of our city rather than that of Philip—provided you yourselves are willing to do your duty, even though it is only to a small extent. For I can see that there are many reasons why Heaven should favour you rather than Philip with her good will. §23 Yet, it seems to me, we sit idly by, doing nothing. And you cannot give instructions to your friends[29]—much less to Heaven—to act on your behalf if you play the sluggard. It is not surprising that Philip has the upper hand: he serves on campaign and toils hard in person, is present on the spot in every situation, and lets pass by no chance or opportunity, while

---

[28] The low opinion held generally by the ancient world of actors, comics and the like is well known (cf. for example, Arist. *NicEth* IV, esp. 8; Dem. XVIII.262). On the low status of public slaves, Aes. I.54. Nothing is known elsewhere of Callias.

[29] We cannot be certain whether 'friends' is meant non-specifically or refers to the Olynthians. If the latter, it is a useful term, as Olynthus is not yet an *ally* of Athens; they have not yet concluded a formal alliance (*symmachia*; compare II.2, I.2, 10 with III.7), although Olynthus has expressed friendship (*philia*) and asked for alliance (Dem. XXIII.109). It is noteworthy that in the first two *Olynthiacs* D. does not ask for help for the Olynthians; he merely urges the Athenians to take advantage of the situation for their own benefit (II.1-2, 26, 31; I.2, 7, 9, 11, 15; compare III.2, 7-8, 16, where sympathy for the new allies is used as a motive; however, III.6, 9).

The Spectre of Philip

you procrastinate, vote decrees and make inquiries. It does not surprise me at all. The opposite, indeed, would be surprising if we, who do none of the things men at war ought to do, should get the better of him who does everything.[30]

§24 I am however surprised, men of Athens, that, though there was once a time when you stood up against the Spartans on behalf of the rights of the Greeks[31] and refused to gain many advantages for yourselves, when it was open to you to do so, but instead preferred to spend your own money in the form of war-taxes and to stand on campaign in the vanguard of danger, that the rest might gain their rights, you now shrink from going out on service and hesitate to pay the war-tax for the sake of your own personal possessions; and that after saving the other Greeks on many occasions—all of them collectively[32] or individually, by turn—you now sit idly by, when you have lost your own possessions. §25 This does surprise me, as, moreover, does the fact that none of you, men of Athens, is able to work out how long a time you have been at war with Philip and reckon up what you have been doing while this time has slipped by.[33] For you must be aware that all this time has slipped past while we have been procrastinating, hoping that others would act, blaming one another, initiating prosecutions,[34] again living in hopes—in fact, doing almost exactly the same as we are doing at this moment. §26 Again, are you so ignorant, men of Athens, as to hope that the city's bad position will be made good by means of the very same activities whereby it was turned from a good into a bad position? This is neither reasonable nor natural. It is much easier in every case to protect what possessions you have than to gain new ones. But now the war has left us none of our former possessions to watch over; and so we

---

[30] Cf. Libanius' Introduction to Speech IV; Dem. IV.2.

[31] D. may have in mind here any or all of the possibilities cited in a note to IV.3, above.

[32] 'Collectively' appears to refer to the Athenian part in the resistance to the Persian invasion, especially at Marathon and Salamis.

[33] The war, of course, has been in progress for 8 years, and Athens' only effective action to date has been the expedition to Thermopylae in 352 (DS XVI.38.1-2; Dem. IV.17, XIX.84; and Just. VIII.2.8-12).

[34] Cf. IV.46-47 and notes. Sealey, *REG* 1955, 93, suggests (on the evidence of schol. Dem. II.25) that D. is referring obliquely to an impeachment of Chares. However, although such an impeachment may have taken place—which would explain, as Sealey says, the absence of Chares from the second expedition to Olynthus (Philochorus F 49-51, our Appendix, 'Selection of Historical Fragments')—it must have been after this speech was delivered, for several reasons. For example, D. refers only to 'generals' (§27), never to one general. Also, as the first of the expeditions to Olynthus was not dispatched until after the delivery of *Olynthiac* III (Cawkwell, *CQ* 1962, 130-4), D. cannot have known about it at this time. For the full arguments, Ellis, *Historia* 1966, 297-301.

must gain new ones. This therefore is the task that is ours right now.³⁵ §27 And so I say that you must contribute money to the war-tax,³⁶ you must yourselves go out on service willingly and you must blame nobody until you have mastered the situation. Then you must honour those deserving of praise and punish those who wrong you, making your judgements on the basis of deeds actually done; and you must do away with excuses and deficiencies on your part. For you have no right to examine stringently the actions of others unless you first have shown yourselves to be doing your duty. §28 For why do you think, men of Athens, that all the commanders you send out—if one must tell something of the truth about the commanders too—why do you think they avoid this war and find private wars of their own? Because in the areas to which we send them the prizes for which the war is fought are yours (thus, if Amphipolis is captured, you will immediately take it over for yourselves),³⁷ whereas the hazards belong personally to the commanders and pay is non-existent;³⁸ but in the wars they find for themselves the hazards are fewer and the pickings belong to the commanders and the soldiers—Lampsacus, Sigeum and the merchant-vessels which they plunder.³⁹ And so each force of mercenaries makes its way towards that which is of advantage to itself. §29 You, however, when you give your attention to the parlous state of your affairs, put your commanders on trial;⁴⁰ and when you have granted them a hearing and have listened to the constraints I have mentioned you acquit them. Therefore, the consequence for you is that while you are quarrelling and at loggerheads with one another—some being convinced of this course of action, others of that—the public welfare suffers. For formerly, men of Athens, you used to pay the war-tax by *symmories*, but nowadays you conduct your politics by *symmories*. A politician [lit.: 'orator'] is leader of each group. Under him he has a general and a claque; these are the 300. The rest of you have been divided up⁴¹ some to this group, others to

---

³⁵ Note D.'s assumption of Athens' 'divine right' (§22) to acquire territory. Cf. §8 and note for his criticisms of Philip for attempting to do the same. Alternatively, in a vague admonition to accept alliance with Olynthus, he may be referring loosely to that city as a 'possession'.
³⁶ Cf. note to IV.7.
³⁷ That is, the mercenaries would not be permitted to plunder it.
³⁸ Although mercenaries were probably underpaid and were expected to augment their allowances with plunder, it is unlikely that as a general rule they were not paid at all, if this is what D. means. Cf. Parke, pp. 144ff.
³⁹ In 355, after his lack of success to date in the Social War, Chares did just what D. condemns here (IV.24 and notes). It was probably at this time that be plundered Sigeum and Lampsacus (Nepos *Chabrias* III.4, Arr. I.12.1, dated by a scholiast on III.31, Ddf. p. 134, *ll.* 20-22). For attacks on commerce, VII.25.
⁴⁰ Cf. IV.47 and notes.
⁴¹ Or 'have divided yourselves up'.

The Spectre of Philip

that.[42] §30 You must drop this practice; you must become your own masters right away and make deliberation, discussion and action matters of common concern. If you allow some to issue orders as though they possessed despotic power over you, others to be compelled to act as trierarchs, to pay the war-tax and to serve on campaigns, and yet others to pass decrees against these people without participating in the general struggle in any way whatsoever, then you will never get anything that is necessary done at the proper time. For the aggrieved section of the community will always let you down and then you will have to punish them instead of your enemies.[43]

To sum up briefly, my proposals are these: everyone must pay a fair amount of the war-tax each from what he possesses; everyone must go out on campaign in turn until you have all done service; you must grant a hearing to all who come forward to speak, and choose, not what so-and-so, or such-and-such a man says, but the best out of all the proposals you hear. If you do this you will praise not only the speaker there on the spot but also yourselves in the future, since your situation in general will be improved.

---

[42] Since 358/7 the war-tax had been paid by a system of *symmoriai* (navy-boards); Philochorus F 41, our Appendix, 'Selection of Historical Fragments'; Arist. *Ath.Pol.* 61.1; Dem. XLVII.21-22. The 1,200 richest citizens were divided into 20 symmories, each of 60 men, each symmory being led by its richest member, the *hegemon* (leader). The 300 richest (sometimes referred to simply as 'the 300') of the 1,200 seem to have formed the first, second and third 'classes' of the symmories, 15 to each board. Our information, however, is sparse on detail; cf. Dem. XVIII.103, 171. In each symmory the *hegemon* was assisted by an *epimeletes* (director or manager). In D.'s none-too-close parallel here, the orator is equated to the *hegemon*. Now that the functions of general and politician were no longer combined in the one person (as they were commonly in the fifth century; e.g., Themistocles, Pericles, Nicias, Alcibiades, Cleon, etc.), except in a few cases such as that of Phocion, the two had to form an alliance (Plut. *Mor.* 486D). Thus it is reasonably accurate to equate *epimeletes* and *strategos*. The rest of the 300, in this analogy, corresponds to the orator's claque. (More accurately, of course, one-twentieth of the 300 should equal the claque.) The remaining members of the 60 in each symmory are vaguely similar to the general supporters of the orator. Cf. Jones, p. 131.

[43] The conclusion D. draws from his analogy may be just, although by those who 'issue orders as though they possessed despotic powers over you' he undoubtedly means those orators whose policies have more appeal than his own. However, political control in the fourth century does seem to have rested largely in the hands of 'politicians', the term including orators and their supporters (cf. Perlman, *Athenaeum* 1963, 328-33; Jones, pp. 127-31).

TRANSLATION AND COMMENTARY
Olynthiac I—August/September(?) 349

§1 If someone were to reveal to you what would benefit the city in the matters you are now discussing, men of Athens, I think you would rather have that than a large fortune. This being so, it is right that you be willing to give an eager hearing to those who desire to counsel you. For while you might listen to and accept the opinion of someone who has come along with a carefully considered and useful plan,[1] I also regard it as a part of your inherent good fortune[2] that some people may be inspired to propose on the spur of the moment many of the things that are in line with our needs; and thus from all the suggestions the choice of what is in your best interest becomes a simple matter.

§2 The present crisis,[3] men of Athens, all but cries out with a human voice that you yourselves must take a firm grasp on the situation there,[4] if indeed you are really concerned about its safety. But what our attitude is towards the situation remains something of a mystery to me. This is what I, at any rate, think you should do. You must vote assistance right now; you must make preparations as quickly as possible, to send a relief force from Athens—and please see to it that the same thing as happened previously does not occur again;[5] and you must send an embassy to

---

[1] 'Carefully considered' as opposed to *ex tempore*. D. himself always prepared his speeches carefully, probably because of his nervousness. Cf. Aes. II.34-35 for the most striking example.

[2] Cf. §10, below, II.1, 10, IV.12. D., in common with most proponents of war, believes the gods to be on the side of 'Right'—that is, on his own side.

[3] Cf. §5, below. The implication here, as elsewhere in *Olynthiacs* II and I (II.2, I.10), is that there is as yet no alliance, although the Olynthians have requested one (cf. III.6-7, where it seems the alliance is in force; the question then is no longer whether to help but how much help to send).

[4] 'There' refers either to the north generally or specifically to Olynthus. If the former, the interests of Athens are mainly two: the Chersonese and Amphipolis. The immediate preparations advocated are very doubtful policy. Could Athens possibly provide large enough forces to compel Philip to meet them? Otherwise, the army might wait indefinitely until Philip should choose to face it. Such a result would cripple Athens financially; cf. Cawkwell, CQ 1962, 132-40.

[5] The previous occasion referred to is very possibly that cited in III.4-5, when an expedition was voted but delayed until too late for effective action then cancelled. But cf. also IV.19 and note.

announce all this and to be there on the spot. §3 For the fellow is a rascal and is clever at turning things to his own advantage[6]—now, it may be, yielding, now threatening (and his threats, with good reason, may be taken at face value) and now misrepresenting us and the fact that we are not on the spot.[7] Thus, my particular fear is that he may turn suddenly and gain for himself, to our disadvantage, something of vital consequence.[8] §4 However, men of Athens, it may reasonably be demonstrated that the one thing among Philip's circumstances that makes him an extremely difficult opponent is also the greatest advantage that you possess. For he is in sole control of all he does, both overtly and secretly; at the same time, he alone is general, master and treasurer; and wherever his army goes, he goes too in person. All this gives him a big advantage in getting warlike enterprises carried out swiftly and at the right time,[9] but the opposite is the case when it comes to reconciliations such as he would be glad to make with the Olynthians. §5 For it is obvious to the Olynthians that they are now fighting not for glory nor for a part of their territory, but about the destruction and enslavement of their country. And they know what he did to those of the Amphipolitans who handed their city over to him,[10] and what he did to those citizens of Pydna who welcomed him as a friend within their gates. I think too that in general despotism is an object of distrust to free constitutions[11]—especially when the two have a common border. §6 I say then, men of Athens, that you must recognize these points; that you must take into consideration everything else that is appropriate; and that you must be willing both to rouse yourselves to activity and to give your attention now, if ever before, to the war, by contributing money with enthusiasm, by going out on campaign yourselves and by leaving nothing undone.[12]

[6] Cf. II.5-8, IV.31, etc.
[7] The diplomatic skirmishes implied here are unknown to us. The question of Philip's 'misrepresentation' of the Athenians' absence from the north is intriguing but very vague. It may consist of accusations of cowardly malingering on the occasions cited and explained in IV.31, 35, or of failing to prosecute the war against him in earnest.
[8] D. is concerned that Philip may regain the Olynthian alliance that D. is seeking for Athens (which may suggest that Philip began this war against his will).
[9] The great advantage of the autocrat; cf. XVIII.235. But D. has perhaps oversimplified the basis of Philip's power; cf. DS XVI.35.2. Aymard, *RIDA* 1950, 61-97, gives the best study to date of the Macedonian kingship.
[10] This does not square with Diodorus' account of Philip's treatment of Amphipolis (XVI.3.3, 8.2), where his consideration towards all but the anti-Macedonian party is stressed. As the Macedonian/Chalcidian alliance of winter 357/6 was formed very shortly after the Amphipolis affair, it would appear that nothing was done which could disenchant the Olynthians at that stage.
[11] For the tendency for Greek states to think of each other in terms of constitutions, that is, to place others in ideological 'pigeon-holes', MacMullen, *G&R* 1963, 118-22, with refs.
[12] Cf. IV.7 and note.

Translation and Commentary: Olynthiac I

For you no longer have any excuse or pretext for being reluctant to do your duty. §7 For now the thing that everyone previously kept on repeating—that the Olynthians must be incited to war against Philip—has come about of its own accord, and that too in a way that above all is to your advantage. For if the Olynthians had taken on the war as a result of your persuasion they would perhaps be shaky allies and would perhaps have resolved on this course only to a certain degree. But as it is, their hatred of Philip stems from the complaints he has made against them,[13] and therefore it is likely that the enmity they feel towards him, because of what they fear and what they have suffered, will be firm and enduring.

§8 Such an opportunity, men of Athens, you must not let slip now that it has fallen into our lap; you must not let the same thing happen to you as has already happened on many occasions in the past. For if, on the occasion when we had returned to Athens after helping the Euboeans, and there were present in the city to speak from this very rostrum the Amphipolitan envoys Hierax and Stratocles, bidding us to sail and take over their city,[14] if we had been ready then to show the same enthusiasm for our own interests as we displayed for the safety of the Euboeans, you would have occupied Amphipolis there and then and would have been relieved of all your subsequent troubles. §9 Again, when the news came that siege was being laid to Pydna, to Potidaea, to Methone, to Pagasae and—so as not to waste time with a full and detailed list—to all the other places,[15] if we had gone then enthusiastically and in a fitting manner in person to the first of these places which asked for aid, we should now be finding Philip an easier and much more

---

[13] The nature of these complaints is unknown, unless D. means the warnings (and more?) Philip gave them in 351 after their peace-overtures to Athens (§13 and note, below). Cf. also Just. VIII.3.10.

[14] The short, successful and easy Euboean campaign took place in about August 357 (DS XVI.7; Dem. VIII.74-5; Aes. III.85; Tod No. 153; on the date Beloch III.1.222). Amphipolis fell some time later, perhaps after two or three months (with Beloch III.1.229, III.2.458) or in the winter of 357/6 (with DS XVI.8, who synchronizes it with the early months of the Social War, for the date of which *see* Cawkwell, *G&M* 1962, 134-40). Dem. VII.27 implies that Athens sent no help because of Philip's (untrustworthy) reassurances, but this seems too weak a reason for Athens' missing an *invitation* to take over what had eluded her for so long. With the winter 357/6 date, Athens would have been unable to help (a) because of her commitment to the war and (b) because of the impossibility of reaching Amphipolis quickly in winter (IV.31).

[15] Pydna fell shortly after Amphipolis, Potidaea in June/July 356, Methone in 354 and Pagasae in 352 (cf. IV.4 and notes for the first three; also §12, below. Beloch III.1.476-7, III.2.267-8, dates the occupation of Pagasae to 353, Hammond, *JHS* 1937, 65-7, to early winter 354, but Ehrhardt, *CQ* 1967, shows that it must be dated with or just after the fall of Pherae, that is, probably in early summer 352).

The Spectre of Philip

humble person to deal with. As it is, men of Athens, by always throwing away the present opportunity and by thinking that the future will automatically turn out well, we ourselves have increased the power of Philip and we ourselves have raised him to a greatness that no other king of Macedonia has yet attained.[16]

But now an opportunity has come of its own accord to the city—that presented by the Olynthian situation—which is as great as any of our previous opportunities. §10 And it seems to me, men of Athens, that if a man were to set himself to give a fair reckoning of the benefits that the gods have shown us, he would express great gratitude to them—and rightly so—even though much is not as it should be. For the fact that we have incurred great losses in the course of the war can justly be put down to our own negligence; but that we did not incur these losses a long time ago and that there has appeared for us an alliance to counterbalance them—if we will make use of this alliance—all this I at any rate would put down as a benefaction stemming from Heaven.[17] §11 Yet the situation is very similar, I feel, to what happens in the acquisition of money: if you save all you acquire, you are filled with a deep sense of gratitude to fortune, but if you spend it without noticing, then you use up at the same time all memory of fortune's favours. So it is with politics: those who have not made proper use of their opportunities have no recollection of any benefit at all received from Heaven. For it is with reference to the final outcome that men make an assessment of each of the things they have formerly enjoyed. Therefore, men of Athens, it is of extreme importance that you take thought for the future course of events, in order that by using these correctly we may wipe out the discredit of our past actions.

§12 And, men of Athens, if we abandon these people too and then Philip subdues Olynthus, what is there, let someone tell me, to prevent him marching where he will?[18] Is there any one of you, men of Athens, who reasons out and considers the manner in which Philip, who was weak at the outset, has grown to greatness? First he seized Amphipolis, then Pydna, then Potidaea followed by Methone, then he set foot in Thessaly. §13 After this came Pherae, Pagasae and Magnesia.[19] He

---

[16] Cf. IV.2-12.
[17] Cf. II.8, 26 and notes, IV.45.
[18] Cf. III.8-9 and note. Here is the difference between the policies of D. and those of Eubulus. D. wants to finish the war while it is yet at a distance—regardless of the limits of finance and of strategic considerations—while Eubulus, more realistically, attempts to conserve Athens' resources for emergencies such as Philip's advance on Thermopylae in 352 (IV.17 and note).
[19] For Amphipolis (followed shortly by the fall of Pydna), Potidaea, Methone, Pagasae and Pherae *see* §9 and note, above. Philip's settlement of Magnesia was in 353 or 352, around the time of the two campaigns against the Phocians; cf. II.11, Isoc. *Philippus* 21, §22 below, Westlake, p. 179, Sordi, p. 266.

settled them all exactly as he wanted and went off to Thrace.[20] There he expelled some of the rulers and others he placed on their thrones. Then he fell ill.[21] On his recovery he did not lapse into idleness, but immediately made his assault on Olynthus.[22] I pass over in silence his campaigns against the Illyrians, the Paeonians, Arybbas and anywhere else that we might mention.[23]

§14 But, someone might say, why are you telling us all this now? I tell you, men of Athens, in order that you may understand and perceive two things: firstly, how unprofitable it is always to sacrifice your political interests one after the other, and secondly, how restless and meddlesome is the activity which is a natural part of Philip's way of life, and which makes it impossible for him to rest quietly content with his achievements. Now, if it is Philip's firm resolve that he must always do something greater than he has already done, and if it is our resolve that we must not apply ourselves with determination to any of our concerns, just consider what outcome we can expect from this situation. §15 By Heaven, which one of you is so simple as not to realize that the war in the north will come here if we do nothing about it?[24] Indeed, men of Athens, if this happens, I am afraid that, just as those who lightly borrow money at a high rate of interest enjoy a brief spell of affluence then later find themselves without even their original capital, so it may become obvious that we too have borrowed our idleness at a high rate of interest; and I fear that by making pleasure the sole object of all our activities we may later be forced to do many of those unpleasant things

[20] Cf. IV.17 and note. The reorganization of tribal Thrace suggested here is a tantalizing reference; we know little or nothing of Philip's achievements in this regard.
[21] Cf. IV.10-11, III.4-5 and note.
[22] The immediate sequel to the Thracian campaign, ending with the unfinished siege of Heraion Teichos (III.4-5) was the *immediate* assault, or attempt, on Olynthus. Some not-so-recent scholars took this to refer to the 349/8 campaign but it has been clearly established as belonging to an earlier affair (cf. Sealey, REG 1955, 83-9 for a statement and rebuttal of the argument. Sealey however sees the affair merely as a 'demonstration' (as also Glotz and Cohen III, p. 279 and CAH VI, 228)). Its cause, whether it was an active attempt or assault, as D. here seems to say, or a warning, as Theopompus F 127 and our Appendix, 'Selection of Historical Fragments' perhaps implies, is undoubtedly to be found in the Olynthian overtures of friendship made to Athens not long before (XXIII.108-109). On the dating cf. also Ellis, REG 1966, 636-9.
[23] Arybbas was king of Epirus and uncle of Olympias, the most prominent of Philip's several wives. For his overthrow by Philip in 342 and the installation of Alexander, Olympias' brother, in his place, see Just. VIII.6.4-8, IG II² 1.226; also Just. VIII.6.11-12, Treves, AJPh 1942, 129-53. However the occasion of the present reference is unknown. For campaigns against the Illyrians and Paeonians in 359 and 358, then again in 356, cf. DS XVI.1.5, 2.4-6, 4.1-7, 8.1, 22.3; Tod No. 157; Just. XII.16.6; Plut. Al. III.5; Beloch III.1.231.
[24] Cf. §12 and note, above.

The Spectre of Philip

we did not want to do and that we may find our position in Attica itself in danger.

§16 Now someone might well object that to indulge in reproach is easy and that anyone can do it; but the task of a councillor is to show what must be done about the present situation. I am well aware, men of Athens, that if something turns out contrary to your wishes you frequently direct your wrath not at the real culprits but at those who were the last to speak on the situation. Nevertheless I do not think that out of consideration for my personal safety I should shrink from expressing my opinion on what I think is to your advantage.[25] §17 I say then that you must save the situation in two ways: by rescuing their cities for the Olynthians, sending out soldiers to do this; and by ravaging Philip's country by means of triremes and troops other than those sent to Olynthus. §18 If you neglect either of these I fear your campaign will be in vain.[26] For if, whilst you are ravaging Macedonia, Philip stays his ground and reduces Olynthus, he will then march off to his own country and repel you without difficulty. Whereas, if you send a relief force only to Olynthus, Philip will settle down to the siege of the city, while at the same time keeping his eye on the situation at home, and in time will overcome the besieged. The relief-force we send, then, must be considerable and in two parts.

§19 This, then, is my opinion with regard to the sending of a relief-force. But what about the provision of funds? You have, men of Athens, you have—I repeat—money in quantities unequalled by other peoples. But you appropriate this money just as you want. If you give this money to the men on active service, you have no need for further revenue,[27]

[25] Cf. IV.51, III.32 and notes.
[26] Reminiscent of the two expeditions proposed in *Philippic* I. The difficulties remain: a force sent to Olynthus, unless it is large enough to march thence to Macedon, must wait indefinitely until Philip takes the initiative or return to Athens with nothing accomplished (the dilemma in fact faced by the three expeditions eventually sent; Philochorus F 49-51, our Appendix, 'Selection of Historical Fragments', with Cawkwell, CQ 1962, 130-4); another to Macedonia itself must be large enough to draw and attack Philip's main army on its own territory, or it can do no more than ravage coastal areas (which were not essential to the Macedonian economy in any case; IV.32 and note) while avoiding his force. There are two serious flaws in D.'s strategy: that Athens has not the strength to defeat Philip on his own ground by themselves and that they have no guarantee of Olynthian loyalty under pressure—as indeed they found out when the city was betrayed to Philip from the inside; XIX.263-267.
[27] The definite character of this reference to the Theoric Fund must lead us to challenge those (e.g. Jones, pp. 33-4) who assume that the only monies controlled by the Theoric Commission are those distributed as festival-dole; cf. my Appendix, *The Theorikon*. However it is also impossible, it would seem, that a fund containing only the surplus above normal State expenditure (Dem. LIX.4) could finance the expeditions proposed; cf. assessment of cost, §20 and note, below.

otherwise, you do need additional revenue—or rather you are without revenue at all. 'What's this?' someone will probably protest. 'Are you proposing that this money be put in the military fund?'[28] Good lord, not I![29] §20 For while I think that soldiers must be equipped [and that this money should be put in the military fund][30] and that there must be one and the same system for taking one's due and for doing one's duty,[31] your way of thinking is that you should receive the money to spend on your festivals, as you do now, without any trouble to yourselves. The only course left open to us, in my opinion, is for all to make contributions—if we need a lot of money, large contributions, if we need a small amount of money, small ones.[32] But we do need money, and without it we cannot do anything that we ought to do. Different people propose various other ways of raising funds; choose whichever of them seems to be to your advantage. But while you have the opportunity, take a firm grasp on the situation.

§21 It is not unrewarding to think about and consider the present state of Philip's affairs. For his affairs at the moment are not in such a state of preparedness and in such an excellent condition as might appear to be the case and as an uncritical observer could well say is the case;[33] nor would Philip ever have begun the war had he thought he would have to fight it. He expected that he would carry all before him by his mere approach—and in that he was mistaken.[34] That this, first of all, has happened, contrary to his expectations, is disturbing him and causing him no little despondency. Then there is the Thessalian situation. §22 The Thessalians, I feel, have invariably been found by all mankind to be naturally untrustworthy,[35] and now, where Philip is concerned,

[28] On the military fund *see* Cawkwell, *Mnemosyne* 1962, 377-83.
[29] For the reason for D.'s unwillingness to act *see* my Appendix, *The Theorikon*.
[30] The words in brackets are regarded by most editors as an interpolation.
[31] Cf. III.34 and note.
[32] As D. does not specify the size of the forces he proposes, we have no idea of the amount of money needed. But on the analogy of those of IV.16, 20-21, and calculating on the costs cited in IV.28-29, we may surmise that the whole expedition would cost no less than 500 talents per annum, requiring an unprecedented 8% *eisphora* (*see* Jones, p. 29 for estimates of the normal levies).
[33] D. presents no evidence to demonstrate that this is *not* the case; this is an unsubstantiated claim advanced probably with a view more to encouragement than to accuracy. We are not well enough informed on Macedon's state of readiness or on her economy to contradict D. outright, but the constant ability of Philip to put an army into the field whenever necessary suggests that the orator is ill-informed or untruthful.
[34] The implication that Philip makes gestures without being willing to back them with action D. contradicts many times; cf., for example, IV.5-6, 34-35, 40-41, II.15, I.4, etc.
[35] Compare with II.7, 11, where the Thessalians are treated as seduced innocents. On the basis of this apparent shift in viewpoint Sordi, p. 264, argues for the

The Spectre of Philip

they are exactly as they have always been. For they have voted to demand Pagasae back from him and have prevented his fortifying Magnesia. And I have heard from certain quarters that they will no longer grant him the enjoyment of the revenues of their harbours and markets.[36] For, they say, the Thessalian Federation should be administered from these revenues; they should not go into Philip's pocket. If Philip is deprived of these funds, he will be extremely hard put to keep up the maintenance of his mercenaries.[37] §23 Moreover, we must believe that the Paeonian, the Illyrian and, in general, all such people would prefer to be autonomous and free rather than slaves.[38] For they are not used to being subject to anyone, and the fellow is an overbearing tyrant, so people say—and, by Heaven, this is perhaps not at all incredible, for in the case of men who lack mental balance and reason, unmerited success can lead to serious errors of judgement. This is why it often appears more difficult to maintain than to obtain one's advantages.

§24 Therefore, men of Athens, you must look upon Philip's lack of opportunity as your opportunity; you must be ready to help the Olynthians to shoulder their burden; you must send embassies where the need arises;[39] you must serve in the army yourselves; and you must stir up everyone else to do the same. For look at the situation like this: if Philip should gain such an opportunity against us and if there were war on our very border, how ready do you imagine Philip would be to march against you? Then, does it not make you feel ashamed if, when you have the opportunity, you lack the resolution to do to Philip the things that Philip would do to you if he were able?

§25 And furthermore, men of Athens, you ought not to overlook the

---

traditional order of the *Olynthiacs*. However, cf. Ellis, *Historia* 1967, 108-11, esp. 111 for a discussion of this point.

[36] Cf. II.11 and note. A comparison suggests strongly that II.11 was spoken before I.22 (Ellis, *Historia* 1967). That there is no mention of the Thessalian situation where we would expect it in *Olynthiac* III suggests, as Sordi has noted, pp. 263-5, that Philip had resolved the difficulty before the time of its delivery, possibly by the reiteration of former promises (II.7 and note), perhaps by threats.

[37] Cf. IV.34 and note.

[38] Cf. IV.4. We know nothing of the measures Philip took to keep these barbaric neighbours in check. In his time there was a Macedonian commandant in Thrace (Berve I.227), and it may be that there were strategically placed armies of occupation in the countries west and north-west of Macedonia, but there is no evidence for this. We are perhaps safer in assuming that the comparative peace was preserved by treaty, threat (DS XVI.22.3 with Tod No. 157; or was this a battle? Plut. *Al*. III.8) and marriage-alliance (?Satyrus, through Athenaeus XIII.557BCD)—that is, after the initial campaigns of 359-356; cf. §13 and note, above.

[39] Cf. II.11.

Translation and Commentary: Olynthiac I

fact that you now have to choose whether you are to fight Philip in the north or Philip is to fight you here. For if the Olynthians hold out, you will fight the war in the north and you will ravage Philip's territory, while enjoying in security this country you now possess and which is your own. But if Philip seizes Olynthus, who will stop him from marching on Attica?[40] §26 The Thebans? It may be a very harsh thing to say, but they will be only too ready to join an invasion of Attica.[41] The Phocians then? Why, they cannot even protect their own country without your assistance.[42] Some other state then?[43] 'But my good man', comes the objection, 'Philip won't want to invade us.' In that case, it would be extremely strange if he did not, when he has the power, do what he now keeps on talking about, laying himself open to a charge of folly. §27 However, I think that no further argument is needed for you to see how great are the differences involved in your fighting the war in Attica from your fighting it in the north. For if you by yourselves had to stay outside the city for only a month and had to take from the produce of the country only as much as men in camp receive—I mean, if there is no enemy in the country—the farming section of your community would, I think, have losses inflicted on them that are greater than all the money you have spent on the war to date. But if a war comes to Attica, how great, do you think, our losses must then be? Besides this factor, there is the arrogance of the invader and, still more, the sense of shame at our position; and this, at least in the opinion of men of intelligence, is worse than any financial loss.

§28 We must all, then, take a comprehensive view of all these points and send out a relief-force and thrust back the war to the north. The wealthy must do this in order that, by spending a small amount of the great wealth they quite rightly possess, they may enjoy the remainder in security; the men of military age in order that, by gaining experience of warfare in Philip's country, they may become formidable guardians of their own—and unravaged—country; and the politicians in order that the account they must submit of their political activities may cause them

---

[40] Cf. III.8-9 and note.
[41] This may well be so, particularly after the Euboean campaign of 357 (cf. 8 and note, above). The most convenient survey of Thebes and her dealings with Athens at this time is in Cloché, *Thèbes de Béotie*, Chapter IX, esp. p. 176.
[42] A reference no doubt to the alliance sought with Athens, Sparta, etc., in the Sacred War (DS XVI.23, 24, 27.3-5). D., as an Athenian, refers in a neutral sense to the Phocian position, rather than in the extremely critical manner we would expect of a Theban or a Thessalian, for example. Cf. Just. VIII.1.4-11 for a partial justification of the Phocian side of the dispute; also DS XVI.23.5, 57. For a condemnation of the Athenian and Spartan part, Just. VIII.2.8-12.
[43] Or, following Blass' punctuation: ' . . . without your assistance or that of some other State'.

The Spectre of Philip

no difficulties.[44] For your judgement of what they have done will itself depend on the kind of situation that encompasses you. On every account, I pray that this situation will be a happy one.

---

[44] D.'s implication that the politicians submit to a *euthyna*—'audit' is to be taken metaphorically. At the end of a magistrate's term of office he was subject to an audit undertaken by *logistai*—'auditors'; cf. Arist. *Ath.Pol.* 48.3, 54 with Jones, p. 101, Aes. III.15; Dem. XVIII.117, 229; *IG* II^2 956. Although in the fourth century political orators became a clearly defined group (Perlman, *Athenaeum* 1963, 327-55), they were quite distinct from magistrates. Although the politician, then, was not subject to audit, it was possible for him to be called to account for his actions by normal process of law—but only when he made illegal proposals or proposals injurious to the State. However, D. is clearly not thinking of this type of case—he is merely using a convenient metaphor.

TRANSLATION AND COMMENTARY
Olynthiac III—c. September(?) 349

§1 I am inspired, men of Athens, with very different thoughts when I consider the speeches that I hear. For I see that while the speeches made are concerned with the punishing of Philip your affairs have reached such a state that we have to consider how we ourselves can avoid being the first to be hurt. It seems to me, therefore, that the people who say such things are making a mistake, precisely in that the subject they are putting forward for your discussion is based on quite false premises. §2 Now I too am quite well aware that there was once a time when it was possible for the city both to keep her own possessions in safety and to take vengeance on Philip. For both these possibilities have occurred in my lifetime, not long ago.[1] Now, though, I am convinced that it is sufficient for the present to see to it that we preserve our allies. For when their security has been firmly established then we shall be able also to discuss the questions from whom and in what manner vengeance is to be exacted. But it is futile, I think, to hold any sort of discussion about the end before the beginning has been properly taken care of.[2]

§3 The present crisis above all requires much thought and deliberation. For my part, I think that to give the necessary advice on the present state of affairs is not a very difficult matter; no, my difficulty, men of Athens, lies in knowing *how* I should speak to you on the subject. For I am convinced, from what I know through being present in the assembly and listening to the debates, that the majority of our political objectives have slipped through our fingers rather because of an unwillingness to do our duty than because of failure to comprehend where our duty lies.[3] I ask you then to bear with me if I am forthright in making my proposals, examining my words to see whether I speak the truth; and to do so for this reason, that the future might be more successful. For look and see how our present situation has reached

---

[1] His lifetime, of course (so far, from 383 to 349), has included the growth and height of power of the Second Athenian League—as well as its decline.

[2] Cf. §§8-9 and note, below.

[3] For similar judgements, cf., for example, IV.2, II.3, 11, I.2.6, etc.

The Spectre of Philip

the ultimate in debasement, through the fact that some people address you only with a view to pleasing you.[4]

§4 I think it necessary first to remind you briefly of what has already happened. You remember, men of Athens, when the report came to you 2 or 3 years ago that Philip was laying seige to Heraion Teichos. That was in *Maimakterion*.[5] There were many speeches and much uproar in the assembly and you decreed that 40 triremes should be launched, that the citizens of up to 45 years of age should embark in them[6] and that a property-tax of 60 talents should be levied. §5 Then this year passed by and the month *Hekatombaion* came, then *Metageitnion* and *Boedromion*.[7] In this month you reluctantly dispatched Charidemus, after the celebration of the Mysteries, with 10 empty triremes and 5 silver talents. For when the news reached you that Philip was ill or dead (both these reports came in), you thought there was no longer any occasion to send help and you dismissed the expedition.[8] But this was exactly the right occasion; for if we had then sent help there, as we had voted, and done so with alacrity, Philip, having made his recovery, would not be bothering us now.[9]

[4] Cf. also IV.51.
[5] That is, *Maimakterion* (approximately November) 352.
[6] Cf. IV.21 and note.
[7] That is, in *Boedromion* (approximately September) 351.
[8] Cf. IV.11.
[9] Cf. Preface to Speech IV. The crucial question posed by §§4-5 is that of the duration of Philip's Thracian campaign (and note that D. elsewhere, I.13, mentions other activities besides the siege of Heraion). Opinions differ as to the interpretation of the present two sections; for a statement of the two possible readings, cf. Ellis, *REG* 1966, 636-9. The key sentence is 'For when the news reached you that Philip was ill or dead, . . . you dismissed the expedition.' Which expedition does he mean, that of *Maimakterion* 352 or that of *Boedromion* 351? This Thracian campaign ended with Philip's illness (I.13). Depending on our interpretation of the above sentence is our calculation of this point in time. Did he fall ill at the end of 352 or towards the end of 351? Did the Thracian campaign last a maximum of five months or a maximum of fifteen (each possibility including the march of about 500 miles from Thermopylae, Philip's location in midsummer 352)? Two considerations encourage the latter answer. First, there is no record of an expedition against Philip led by Charidemus at this time (an argument *ex silentio*, of course, and weak by itself), which suggests that it was the one dismissed. Second, the implication is strong that Charidemus was to be dispatched to attack Philip and that he was to attack him (however ineffectively, with his pitiful force) in Thrace, 'there', as D. says. But if Philip left Thrace almost a year before, after his recovery, what was the point in that?

Our reconstruction (based, then, on the assumption that the expedition dismissed was the second) is as follows. When the news of the Thracian campaign reached Athens, the first expedition was proposed and voted in the assembly. But when it came to the point of actually paying the property-tax and enrolling for service, the numbers of citizens attempting to avoid this duty (to

§6 However, what was done then cannot be undone. But there has now come an opportune moment for action in another war[10]—and it was because of this that I reminded you of these events, in order that you might not repeat your experiences. How then, men of Athens, shall we make use of this opportunity? For if you do not send help 'with all your strength and to the best of your ability',[11] consider how you will prove to have managed all your military operations on Philip's behalf. §7 At the beginning of the war the Olynthians were in possession of a considerable military strength and the political situation was as follows: Philip had no confidence in the Olynthians and they had none in Philip.[12] We and the Olynthians made a peace with each other;[13] this was like putting a chain on Philip, and it was annoying to him that a large city, which had become reconciled to us, should be lying in wait for the chances he offered.[14] We thought that we ought to do all in our power to involve the Olynthians in war with Philip; and now that which everyone kept on talking about has been effected somehow or other.[15] §8 What then remains for us, men of Athens, except to send help vigorously and eagerly? I see no other course open to us. For apart from the disgrace that would encompass us if we were

which they were committed, perhaps, by a panic-decision or by an unrepresentative crowd in the assembly) delayed the dispatch so considerably that the expedition finally *lapsed* through lack of support (cf. III.14 and Aes. II.37; this could happen), probably before it reached the water. Finally the people were persuaded that action was still necessary, and Charidemus, very inadequately prepared, was given the order (compare IV.19 and note). However, shortly afterwards, on receipt of the news of Philip's illness or death, that expedition was *dismissed* (which may mean dismissed from this particular commission and merely re-routed to the Hellespont for normal service there; we find him 'commander at the Hellespont' in 349; Philochorus F 50, our Appendix, 'Selection of Historical Fragments'). This reconstruction is so close to what D. actually described in IV.36-37 that it is extremely tempting to connect the two directly.

[10] Cf. I.8-9.
[11] This formula, or variations on it, is extremely common in treaties of alliance (e.g., Tod Nos 101 *ll.* 6-7, 103 *ll.* 7(?), 118 *ll.* 24, 27-28, 123 *l.* 51, 127 *ll.* 4-6, 9-10, 16-17, 26-27, etc.). D. may be using it here simply as a common expression or he may be quoting it directly from the newly sworn treaty with Olynthus, to remind his listeners of their obligations under its terms.
[12] As we have seen (II.1 and note), this evaluation of the earlier Olynthian relationship with Philip is over-simplified; as for Philip's confidence in Olynthus, West, *NumChron* 1923, 169-211, has shown what reliance he placed on at least the Chalcidian merchants to build up the economy of his own country.
[13] D. uses the word 'peace' here rather than 'alliance'. He is evidently referring to the initial declaration of peace by Olynthus in 352 (XXIII.108-109), or perhaps to a later, but not extant, confirmation of that peace.
[14] Hence the admonitory (and punitive?) expedition against the Chalcidian cities after the close of the Thracian campaign in late 351 (IV.17, I.13 and notes).
[15] Cf. I.7.

The Spectre of Philip

treacherously to abandon any of our obligations, I can see the consequences of doing this affording us no small cause for fear, with the Thebans feeling towards us the way they do, with the Phocian finances exhausted and with nothing standing in the way of Philip's turning his attention to Attica when he has reduced his present opponents.[16] §9 Indeed, if any one of you is for putting off his duty until that point is reached, he wants to see the terrors of war at close quarters, though it is possible for him to hear about them happening elsewhere; and he wants to look for helpers for himself, although it is now possible for him to send help to others. For I think that almost all of us know that this is how things will turn out if we throw away the present opportunity.

§10 Yes, someone might say, we all know that we must send help, but you tell us how! Well then, men of Athens, do not be surprised if my suggestion is somewhat different from what most of you expect. It is this: set up a legislative commission.[17] When this commission is in session, do not pass any laws at all—for you have quite enough of them —but repeal those laws that are harming you with regard to the present situation. §11 To come right out into the open, I mean the theoric laws[18] and some of the laws dealing with military service, of which

[16] It is illuminating, at this stage, to note the change that has taken place in D.'s stated motives for opposition to Philip over the last 2 years. In 351/50, in his speech *On the Rhodians*, he fleetingly mentions Philip as contemptible (§15). At about the same time (see note below), his full efforts are concentrated against a Macedonian no longer beneath contempt. D. urges action against him, putting forward as motives the recovery of lost possessions, vengeance and the regaining of Athenian pride (IV.7, 9-10, 42, 50; although note the caution in IV.43, 50). Some eighteen months later again, in *Olynthiac* II, much the same motives are apparent (II.2, 24, 26). Very shortly afterwards: the hour is late; attack Philip before he wins Chalcidice and turns to Attica itself (I.2, 11-15, 24-27). Shortly afterwards again, D.'s message is even more urgent: it is too late for vengeance; drastic action is needed; Athens must save her allies and herself; this is the eleventh hour (III.1-2, 8-9, 10-13, 33).

Note. For the dating of the speech *On the Rhodians* cf. Sealey, REG 1955, 188, who supports the Dionysiac date of 351/50. This must be roughly correct, because Artemisia, who died in this year after reigning 2 years, is mentioned (§11), but the precise date is conjectural, depending on D.'s vague reference (§12) to unconfirmed events involving an attack on Egypt by Persia, a campaign apparently lasting about a year; Olmstead, p. 433.

[17] That is, a committee of *nomothetai* (proposers or movers of laws). The system of law-revision is too detailed to discuss fully here, but cf. *OCD* and see 'Nomothetae'; Jones, pp. 52, 122-3; Hignett, *A History of the Athenian constitution to the end of the fifth century B.C.*, Oxford University Press, London 1932, Appendix I, pp. 299-305. The system seems to date from the restoration of the democracy in 403 (Andoc. I.81-84; Harrison, *JHS* 1955, 22ff.), at least in its fourth-century form. The main primary sources are Aes. III.38-40 and Dem. XXIV.17-33.

[18] Cf. my Appendix: *The Theorikon*.

the former distribute the military funds as theoric money to those staying at home and the latter allow those shirking their military obligations to evade punishment,[19] while they further undermine the morale of those who want to do their duty. When you have repealed these laws and made the way safe for speaking what is best,[20] then look for someone to propose what you all know is to your advantage. §12 But until you have done this, do not ask who is willing to speak what is best for you, only to be ruined at your hands. For you will not find anyone, especially as the only outcome will be that whosoever proposes and moves these measures will not only meet with unjust and harmful treatment without helping the situation, but will also make it even more dangerous in the future than it is now to speak what is best. And, men of Athens, you must demand that the same men who set up these laws should also repeal them.[21] §13 For it is not right that the popularity by which the whole State has been harmed should belong to those who then passed the law, while the odium of the action through which we can all fare better should involve in personal loss any man who now gives the best advice. Until you settle these matters, men of Athens, you must in no way think that there is among your number anyone so powerful as to transgress these laws and get away with it unpunished, nor anyone so foolish as to plunge himself into manifest danger. §14 And indeed, men of Athens, you must not be unaware of the fact that a decree is worth nothing if it is not accompanied by the willingness to execute with enthusiasm at least the resolutions it contains.[22] For if decrees were of themselves sufficient either to compel you to do what should be done or to accomplish the things about which they were proposed, then you would not be in the position of passing many decrees, but of executing few—or rather, none at all—of them, and Philip would not have continued his insolence for such a long time.[23] For if decrees counted for anything, he would have

---

[19] This is probably a reference to the practice of a conscripted citizen's providing a substitute to fill his place—perhaps a mercenary or a slave; IV.36, Thuc. VII.13.

[20] Until the laws were changed, the proposer of an illegal motion—for example, to transfer the Theoric Fund to the military fund—was liable to the *graphe paranomon* (cf. my Appendix, *The Theorikon*; Goodwin, *Demosthenes: De Corona*, pp. 316-27).

[21] Undoubtedly a reference to Eubulus (who is closely connected with the establishment of the Theoric Commission; schol. Aes. III.25, Theopompus F 99, our Appendix, 'Selection of Historical Fragments', schol. Dem. X.11, Ddf., p. 203 l. 21) and his followers; Cawkwell, *JHS* 1963, 53-61, esp. 54. D.'s opposition to Eubulus has already been noted (note 2 to Speech IV); he returns to the attack below (§§27-32), on different grounds. Cf. also schol. III.29, Dinarchus I.96; Dem. V.5 and note.

[22] Cf. IV.19, III.4-5.

[23] Ibid.

The Spectre of Philip

paid the penalty long ago. §15 But things are not like this. Action chronologically follows debating and voting, but in its effectiveness it is more important than and superior to both these things. We must then have action—everything else we have already. For, to be sure, men of Athens, you have among your number people who can tell you what is needed and you are unsurpassed in judging what is said; now you will be able, if you act correctly, actually to do something as well.

§16 For what moment, what opportunity do you seek, men of Athens, better than the one you have now? When will you do your duty if not now? Has not the fellow already seized all our territorial possessions,[24] and if he becomes master of this country [Olynthus] shall we not suffer the most shameful fate imaginable? We promised the Olynthians that we would promptly come to their rescue if they went to war. Well then, are they not at war? Is Philip not an enemy? Does he not hold all our strategic positions? Is he not a barbarian?[25] Is he not anything you like to call him? §17 But, in the name of Heaven, when we have let all these things go and when we have practically given Philip a helping hand to get them, shall we then try to seek out the men who are responsible for these disasters? For that we shall not lay the blame before our own door I know full well. Amidst the perils of war none of those who have fled from the field accuses himself; he accuses his commander, his neighbours and everyone, rather than himself. Yet it seems to me that the responsibility for the defeat lies with everyone who ran away. For he who now accuses the others could have stood his ground—and if each man had done this they would have won the day. §18 And so now, suppose someone does not give the best advice; then let another get up and give it, but let him not blame the one who has just spoken. Suppose the second speaker gives better advice; then do as he suggests and good luck to you. But, comes the objection, what he proposes is not pleasant. But this is not the fault of the speaker, unless he neglects to make the requisite prayer.[26] It is an easy matter,

[24] Cf. IV.4, I.9, 12-13 and notes.
[25] Cf. §24, below, IX.31. Although 'barbarian' is not necessarily a term of contempt, it tended to be so, especially after the Persian Wars (Ar. *Clouds* l. 492; Thuc. VIII.98.1; Xen. *Anab.* V.4.34; Dem. XXI.150; compare Kitto, *The Greeks*, Penguin, London 1957, pp. 7-8, who oversimplifies). There can be no doubt of its pejorative use here. There is little point in questioning the justice of its application here to Philip; while some Greeks conceded the Hellenic descent, or at least connections, of the Macedonian royal house and nobility (Hdt. V.22, VIII.137, IX.45), there is no doubt that many would consider tribal Macedonia as non-Greek, or barbarian (cf. Walbank, *Phoenix* 1951, 41-60, but also Andriotes, *Balkan Studies* I, 1960, 143-8; Dascalakis, *The Hellenism of the Ancient Macedonians*, pp. 256-69).
[26] An ironic reference to the habit of some speakers of uttering pious petitions to the gods (as, for example, D. himself does at the beginning of the speech *On the Crown*; XVIII.1-2).

men of Athens, to make prayers, cramming into a few words all that one wants, but it is not so easy to make a choice when affairs of state are put before you for consideration; then you must take the best course in place of the pleasant, if you cannot take both together.

§19 But, someone might say, if anyone can both leave the theoric monies alone and propose for us other ways and means for our military expenses, surely he is a better councillor? I quite agree, men of Athens, if this is possible! But I wonder whether anyone at all, after spending his resources on unnecessary things, ever has been or ever will be in a position to make provision for necessities from what he no longer has. Yet I think that the wish of each individual is to a great extent at the bottom of such proposals—and that is why the easiest thing in the world is self-deception. For each man believes what he wants to be true, which is very often just not the case in affairs of state. §20 Therefore, men of Athens, consider the possibilities of the situation; and consider how you will be able to go out on campaign and how you will receive pay. Surely it is not the part of intelligent or high-minded men to leave undone any of the operations of war because of lack of finance, and to endure with equanimity the reproaches incurred by such conduct; nor is it their part to snatch up arms and march against Corinth and Megara,[27] but to allow Philip to enslave Greek cities because they have no money for the provisioning of the men on active service.

§21 My decision to say these things is not a frivolous one, made for the purpose of quarrelling with certain men among your number. For I am not so foolish or misguided as to want to make enemies for myself when I think that no benefit derives from it. Rather I think it the duty of a right-minded citizen to choose the safety of the city's interests in preference to winning popularity by means of his oratory.[28] Indeed I am told—and perhaps you are too—that the political speakers in the time of our forefathers, men who are praised but little imitated by all who come forward to speak here, adopted this standard and manner of political life—the famous Aristides, Nicias, my own namesake, and Pericles.[29] §22 But from the time that these politicians have appeared on the scene, those who keep asking you 'What is it you wish? What shall I propose? How can I gratify you?', the city's interests have been sacrificed for the popularity of the moment,[30] and the following is the

---

[27] Cf. Philochorus F 155 and Androtion F 30, our Appendix, 'Selection of Historical Fragments'.

[28] Cf. IV.38-39, 51.

[29] On Aristides, cf. for example, Plut. *Arist.* II.4-5, III, Nepos, *Arist. passim*; on Nicias, Plut. *Nicias* III, V; on Demosthenes we have nothing of his popular oratory (but cf. Thuc. IV.10) and know little at all except as regards his military exploits; on Pericles, Thuc. II.65, Plut. *Peric.* V, VII, IX.

[30] Cf. IV.51.

The Spectre of Philip

result: the affairs of these men are flourishing[31] while your own affairs are in a disgraceful state.

§23 And yet, men of Athens, consider what could be said to be the main characteristics of the deeds performed in the days of our forebears and of those done in your own times. What I say will be short and familiar to you, for you can become successful without the need to follow the examples of others; just follow those you have at home. §24 Our forebears, who were neither flattered nor wooed by their politicians, were rulers for 45 years of the Greeks,[32] with their acquiescence.[33] They collected in the Acropolis more than 10,000 talents;[34] they had as a subject the king who then ruled this country we are talking about—as is proper for a barbarian in his relations with Greeks;[35] they set up many fine trophies for victories on land and sea, themselves serving in person on campaign; and alone of mankind they left behind themselves a glory from their achievements superior to the slanders of the envious. §25 This is what they were like in Hellenic affairs; what they were like in domestic affairs, look and see![36] In the public sphere they built for us edifices and beautiful objects of such quality and so many in number—I refer to the temples and the dedicatory offerings in them—that succeeding generations have been left no chance of surpassing them. And in their private lives they were so restrained and so staunchly adherent to the spirit of the constitution §26 that if anyone happens to know the character of the houses of Aristides, Miltiades and the famous men of that time[37] he sees that they are no more magnificent than the houses of their neighbours. For they did not administer the city's affairs to gain a fortune for themselves, but each one of them thought that he should further the common good. And because they conducted the affairs of Hellas with honour, their dealings with Heaven with piety and their domestic affairs with fairness, they

---

[31] §29, below.
[32] II.9 and note, 24.
[33] On the popularity of Athens among her fifth-century allies, Jones, Chapter III, pp. 164-72 (which chapter was first published in 1953), concludes that Athens was no more imperialistic than other similar powers and that her allies had no special reason to dislike her. De Ste Croix, *Historia* 1954/5, 1-41, in agreement with Jones, examines the whole question at length. Recently, however, Bradeen, *Historia* 1960, has attacked this view.
[34] Thuc. II.13.3.
[35] Perdiccas II of Macedon. For 'barbarian' cf. §16 and note, above. It is most misleading to call Perdiccas an Athenian subject; cf. for example, Thuc. IV.132.1, V.6.2, 80.2, VI.7.3-4, VII.9.
[36] Compare §§25-30 with XXIII.207-210 for exactly the same sentiments, in some places expressed in exactly the same words.
[37] Cf. §20 and note, above. This Miltiades is undoubtedly the father of Kimon; cf. Hdt. VI.104, 136-140.

quite rightly gained for themselves great happiness.[38] §27 This, then, is how things were with our forefathers, because they used the leaders I have mentioned. And how do our affairs now stand at the hands of the worthies we have? Are they the same or similar? They indeed ... I have many things that I could say but I pass over them all in silence, except this: you all see how clear of competitors the field had become for us, with the Spartans ruined, the Thebans with their hands full, and of the rest no one state strong enough to take us on in a struggle for the first place.[39] We could both have kept our own possessions with security and have acted as arbiters of the claims of others. §28 Yet we have been deprived of our own territory[40] and have spent more than 1,500 talents on unnecessary objectives,[41] while the allies we gained in time of war have been lost by these politicians in time of peace; and, thanks to the practice we have given him, we have made Philip the powerful enemy that he is. If this is not so, let someone come forward and tell us from what other source than ourselves Philip has derived his strength.[42] §29 But my dear sir, comes the objection, if these things are in a poor state, our domestic affairs are at least in better shape! Yes, and what could we mention to support this? The battlements that we cover in plaster, the roads that we repair, the water-supplies and such idiocies? Look, if you please, at the authors of these pieces of statesmanship![43] Some of them have become rich men after

---

[38] The English language does not do full justice to the word *eudaimonia* (literally: [under the influence of] a good spirit). Our translation 'happiness' conveys only a part of its possible meaning, which took Aristotle the 10 books of the *Nicomachean Ethics* to explore. The word 'blessedness' also conveys some of the connotations of *eudaimonia*. Its approximate counterpart in Latin is *felicitas*.

[39] A reference probably to the period after the Battle of Mantinea of 362, when the weakness of Sparta was confirmed, and when Thebes, despite her success, had lost Epaminondas, her leader and driving-force (Ryder, Chapters V and VI). From the reference to Thebes we see that D. means the Sacred War, but by this time Athens had been involved in and was later exhausted by the Social War.

[40] Cf. IV.4, 5-6 and notes.

[41] An extremely low figure (a conventional estimate, thinks Parke, p. 145; cf. Aes. II.71). Robbins, *CPh* 1918, 361-88, estimates war expenditure for 378-369 at 3,400 to 3,900 talents. Isocrates, VII.9, perhaps exaggerating, claims that 1,000 talents were spent on mercenaries during the Social War. The Thermopylae campaign of 352, lasting only a few weeks, cost 'over 200 talents, including the private expenditure of the men serving' (XIX.84). The 1,500 talents here cited must refer however to other expeditions—D. presumably would not consider the Social War, the Thermopylae campaign and the defence of Olynthus 'unnecessary'; for example, cf. §20 and note, above, V.5.

[42] Cf. IV.2, 17, II.4.

[43] Another reference to Eubulus and his supporters, those whom he has just called 'these politicians' (§28, above; also cf. §12 and note, above). On Eubulus' policy and achievements, Cawkwell, *JHS* 1963, 47-67.

The Spectre of Philip

being beggars, others have risen from obscurity to prominence, and some have provided themselves with private houses on a more magnificent scale than the State buildings. The more the fortunes of the city have decreased, the more their own have increased.

§30 What then is the cause of all these things, and why, do you think, was everything fine in those days but nowadays is all wrong? Because then the people dared to act, and themselves serve on campaign,[44] and so were the masters of their politicians and themselves controlled all the rewards. Each separate individual was content to receive from the people a share in honour or office or any good thing there was. §31 But now the opposite is the case. The politicians control the rewards and everything is managed through them,[45] while you the people, stripped of moral fibre and shorn of your money and allies, have taken the position of a servant and a superfluous appendage, content if they give a share of the theoric monies[46] or if they put on a procession at the Boedromia[47]—yes, and bravest of all, you actually owe them a debt of gratitude for what is your own! They have penned you up in the city; they entice you to these pleasures; and they tame you like animals, making you come and eat from their hands. §32 But I think it is impossible for men whose actions are petty and mean ever to have a great and noble thought. For whatever is the character of men's practices, such must also be the thoughts they have. I would not be surprised, by Demeter, if I received greater harm at your hands for saying these things than the men who have actually brought them to pass. For there is not always free speech allowed on every subject in your assembly; indeed I am amazed that it has happened now.[48]

§33 If then, even now, late as it is, you rid yourselves of these habits and are willing both to serve on campaign and to act worthily of yourselves and to use these surpluses at home as resources for the securing of benefits abroad, then, men of Athens, perhaps you may gain some great

---

[44] Cf. refs to Parke cited in note to IV.24; also II.24.
[45] Cf. II.29.
[46] Cf. I.19-20, III.10-13, my Appendix, *The Theorikon*.
[47] Festival games held annually in *Boedromion* (probably on the seventh day) to commemorate Theseus' victory over the Amazons; Plut. *Thes.* XXVII.
[48] Cf. IV.51, I.16. While at certain times in Athenian history (e.g., 411 BC; Thuc. VIII.65) orators' persons or lives might be in danger, and while Athens was as subject to gang-violence as any other large city (cf. for example, Dem. LIV *passim*), this slur on the character and methods of Eubulus and his followers must be treated with reserve. We have no evidence for the manhandling of orators in D.'s time merely because they have proposed unpopular measures (although they might be liable to a *graphe paranomon* if the measures could be considered illegal; cf. my Appendix, *The Theorikon*; Goodwin, *Demosthenes: De Corona*, pp. 316-27). It is unlikely that D. has anything to fear but unpopularity—and he has already discounted popularity-seeking as an honourable motive in politicians (§§21-22 and note, above).

and lasting good and be rid of petty gains such as these, which may be compared with the diets prescribed by doctors. These diets neither put strength into a man nor allow him to die; likewise, these distributions that you make amongst yourselves are neither large enough to have any lasting benefit, nor do they allow you to give them up and do something else; they just increase the indifference of each one of you. §34 Do you mean payment for services rendered? someone will say. Yes I do, and I mean that we must immediately adopt the same system for everyone, men of Athens, in order that each man may take his due share from public funds and so be ready to do whatever the city requires of him. Supposing it is possible to live in a state of peace; then a man is better off if he stays at home, freed from the necessity of doing something degrading for lack of money. Or supposing there is a situation such as exists at present, for example, then he is in a better position if he serves in person as a soldier, as a man ought to do for the sake of his country, supported by these same sums of money. Suppose that one of you is above the age for military service; he is better off receiving under a fair system, as his pay for overseeing and managing the necessary branches of the administration, the monies he now receives under no system and with no benefit to the city.[49] §35 In a word, I have neither taken money away from you nor added to your expenses save by trifling amounts, but by removing disorder and confusion I have brought[50] the city to a state of order by creating a system

[49] Cf. I.20. §§33-35 contain a puzzling suggestion to follow up the advocated cancellation of the theoric laws (§§10-13 and note, above). D. is not advocating a reversion to the pre-355 system, under which the excess over State expenditure went in war-time to the military fund but in peace-time to the Theoric Commission (my Appendix, *The Theorikon*). He is proposing to abolish the fund completely. All excess monies are to be spent on State pay, it would seem, obviously, in war-time, for the citizen-soldiers, but as well, and especially in peace-time, for *all* those who serve the State in any capacity. This is what the Greek suggests, but what does it mean? From our evidence it appears that all citizens holding State offices were already paid for their services (Ps-Xen. *Ath.Pol.* I.3 with Larsen, *CPh* 1946, 91-8; Arist. *Ath.Pol.* 24.3, 29.5), except in certain emergencies. Does D. mean then that such payment should be increased (it was low enough; Jones, pp. 17-18) with the extra money that would be available? Or perhaps increase the amount available for assembly-meetings, for which enough was provided only to pay the quorum that arrived earliest (Jones, pp. 5-6)? Or is this stretching the meaning too far? Might he intend then that the extra money be used in peace-time to guarantee the State against the sort of situation he warned against in 353 (XXIV.99, or that occurred only a few months after that speech was delivered (XXXIX.17; cf. XLV.4)), when State finances were so depleted during the Euboean expedition that the law-courts were closed for lack of pay for jurors? The difficulty is that the first of these suggestions is apparently the point made by D., and yet that is the only one that seems quite impossible.

[50] 'I have brought.' There is a grammatical ambiguity here. The Greek aorist

The Spectre of Philip

which is the same for receiving money, for serving on campaign, for acting as juror and for doing whatever each man can do, depending on his age and the needs of the situation. Nowhere have I proposed that what belongs to the active citizen should be distributed to those who do nothing, nor that we ourselves should be idle, lazy and helpless while listening to reports of the victories of so-and-so's mercenaries.[51] For this is what is happening now. §36 And I am not blaming the man who is doing your duty for you; I am asking you to do—yourselves for yourselves—those things for which you honour others and not to retreat, men of Athens, from the station of honour that was won for you and left to you by your forebears through so many glorious perils.

I have stated more or less what I think to be to your advantage. May you choose the course that is going to benefit both the city and all of you!

---

might express the English aorist, present or even perfect. Demosthenes, to impress upon the audience the excellence of his proposals, is representing their future results as already having been achieved. Cf. Milns, *Eranos* LXVII, 1969, 208-9.

[51] Cf. IV.20 and note, on mercenaries. Whatever this sentence may refer to—if indeed to any specific occasion—it certainly provides no evidence for placing the first expedition to Olynthus (cf. my Appendix, 'Chronological Table') before this speech, as some have maintained. D. is apparently condemning a fourth-century Athenian habit, not a single aberration of the immediate past.

ON THE PEACE

Speech V

PREFACE TO SPEECH V

Shortly after the delivery of *Olynthiac* III, in September, or perhaps as late as October 349, the first expedition was sent to the Olynthians.[1] Then, with the onset of winter, further aid, even had the Athenians decided to vote it, was impracticable. Early in the new year, a revolt erupted in Euboea, leading the Athenians to send an interim force under the command of Phocion.[2] After a victory at Tamynae, Phocion garrisoned a narrow section of the island. However, when the full citizen-levy arrived, under Molossus, he was recalled. Molossus was singularly unsuccessful, to the extent of being himself captured, and the Athenian forces were forced to retire, the cavalry being sent direct to Olynthus[3] with the second expedition to that city, under Charidemus.

When Philip finally attacked Olynthus, in April, May or even later, there was a final Olynthian appeal, followed by the dispatch of the third expedition, which arrived, thanks probably to the Etesian winds, after Olynthus had fallen.

Philip's treatment of the Olynthians—the allies, it is often overlooked, who turned on him once the prospects of an Athenian alliance seemed hopeful—was severe.[4] Olynthus itself was destroyed and its people sold into slavery and the fortifications of several of its neighbours were removed.[5]

---

[1] For the expeditions *see* the Preface to the *Olynthiacs*, and our Appendix, 'Selection of Historical Fragments' under Philochorus F 49-51. Olynthus itself was not yet under attack and we do not know precisely what action this force took on its arrival.

[2] Which D. opposed; V.5 and notes. Plutarch, followed by several modern writers, thought that Philip was behind this revolt, but cf. Cawkwell, CQ 1962, 129-30.

[3] XXI.197.

[4] Although, as Hammond points out, p. 550, less severe than that recently inflicted by Athens on Sestus; DS XVI.34.3.

[5] DS XVI.53; Dem. IX.56, 66; XIX.267.

Before the fall of Olynthus, Philip had indicated through several sources his desire for peace with Athens.[6] The Athenian, Philocrates, passed a resolution inviting Philip to send envoys to discuss reconciliation, but was attacked for illegality. In the subsequent trial, undoubtedly held before the fall of Olynthus,[7] Philocrates was unable to defend himself, but his defence was conducted successfully by Demosthenes.[8] However, the destruction of Olynthus seems to have frightened the Athenians and there was no more talk of peace until the second half of 347.

Meanwhile, Phocian affairs were complicating matters. In 347, Phalaecus, the Phocian commander, was deprived of his command and replaced by a coterie of generals who, early in 346, asked Athens for aid.[9]

By this time, Eubulus, still a more influential figure in Athens than Demosthenes, had passed a decree sending out heralds to all the Greek states, with a view to forming a general alliance against Philip.[10] Seizing on the Phocian request, the Athenians sent off Proxenus to effect the takeover of some Phocian bases offered by the generals in exchange for the aid, bases which would be extremely important in the feared invasion by Philip of central Greece. However, by the time that Proxenus arrived, Phalaecus had re-secured the command and rescinded the earlier offer.[11] Seeing no chance of effective alliance with Phalaecus, nor of the use of Phocian bases for the defence of Thermopylae and of the alternative route into central Greece, through Phocis, Athens sent off the first embassy of 346, probably in February, to invite Philip's envoys to Athens.[12] This was expedient; there was, however, still the chance of the general Greek alliance, once the heralds returned from the other Greek states.

At the same time as the first embassy left Macedon with Philip's assurances that his own envoys would follow, Philip himself left for Thrace to attack his neighbour, Cersobleptes.[13]

When both groups of envoys had arrived in Athens, but before the heralds had returned from the Greek cities, two special assemblies were held on consecutive days. Two proposals were discussed on the first day: one, put forward by Athens' allies, that peace should be made and

---

[6] Cf. my Appendix, 'Chronological Table', where basic references are cited; also Aes. II.12-17.
[7] Cawkwell, *REG* 1960, 417 n. 2.
[8] Aes. II.12-17.
[9] *See* my Appendix, 'Chronological Table'.
[10] Ibid.
[11] Ibid.
[12] For discussions of the Phocian part in forcing Athens to negotiate, Sealey, *WS* 1955, 145-52; Cawkwell, *REG* 1960, 418-33.
[13] *See* my Appendix, 'Chronological Table'.

Preface to Speech V

that all Greek states have the option of joining this peace within three months, and the alternative, moved by Philocrates, that both peace and alliance should be made with Philip, but that this should be bilateral rather than multilateral. On the second day Demosthenes, president for the day, and acting apparently on information from Philip's envoys, Antipater and Parmenion, that the former motion was not acceptable, came down on the side of Philocrates. The motion was passed by the assembly.[14]

Following this decision, another embassy (the second) was sent off to obtain Philip's signature, but, after a slow trip to Pella, was there delayed even further until Philip returned from Thrace, two months after accepting Cersobleptes' surrender.[15]

Taking the envoys with him, Philip then marched south to Pherae, only a short distance from Thermopylae. Signing the treaty there, he moved on behind the embassy, so that by the time they reached Athens he was in control of the pass.[16] The Athenian assembly, on the motion of Philocrates, confirmed the peace, extending it to Philip's descendants.

Only a few days later, Philip requested Athens to send troops to aid in the subjugation of Phocis. Not wishing to see any extension of his control in central Greece and fearful that it might be a trap, Athens refused, dispatching the third embassy to convey this decision. (As there were no military obligations involved in the treaty, this was no contravention of the peace.) However, before it reached Philip, Phalaecus capitulated and the envoys returned.[17]

Philip then called a meeting of the Amphictyons, to impose terms on Phocis. Aeschines, a member of the (fourth) embassy, representing Athens in Delphi, proposed a moderate solution, in opposition to the extreme penalties insisted on by delegates from some other states.[18] The council, controlled in effect by Philip, through the Thessalian votes,[19] decided to split the Phocian towns into villages, confiscate all weapons and impose an annual indemnity to restore the plundered treasures of the Delphic sanctuary. (This fine was reduced in a few years' time.) The two Phocian votes on the council were transferred to Philip.[20]

---

[14] Ibid. For a full discussion of the assemblies see Cawkwell, *REG* 1960, 433-8 and *CQ* 1963, 120ff.; also *CAH* VI, 233-43.
[15] At Hieron Oros. Cf. my Appendix, 'Chronological Table'. The defeat of Cersobleptes put Philip within easy reach of the Hellespont. That Athens was conscious of the threat is apparent from the dispatch of Diopeithes with colonists to the Chersonese, to strengthen Athenian control there; VIII.6.
[16] See my Appendix, 'Chronological Table'.
[17] Ibid.
[18] Aes. II.142-143.
[19] V.23 and note.
[20] This was in fact a moderate solution, probably agreed to or insisted on by Philip in order to placate Athens.

The Spectre of Philip

The remaining difficulty was to obtain Athens' assent to these decisions. Accordingly, envoys were sent to report the resolutions to the Athenian people, evoking a furious debate in the assembly. However, although they refused to send delegates to the Pythian games, to be chaired by Philip, the Athenians took the sensible line of agreeing to the resolutions.

After the games, Philip returned to Macedon.

The speech *On the Peace* may have been delivered at this last, stormy assembly, but possibly comes later.[21] At any rate, it exemplifies the line taken by the assembly.

---

[21] Libanius' Introduction to Speech V.3 and note.

LIBANIUS' INTRODUCTION TO SPEECH V

§1 As the Amphipolitan war dragged on,[1] both Philip and the Athenians became desirous of peace, the Athenians because they were doing badly in the war,[2] and Philip because he wanted to fulfil the promises he had made to the Thessalians and the Thebans. To the Thebans he had promised to hand over the Boeotian cities of Orchomenos and Koroneia, to both Thebans and Thessalians that he would end the Phocian war.[3] This was impossible as long as the Athenians were at war with him. For, formerly, when he wanted to invade Phocis, the Athenians had sailed their fleet around to the so-called Gates (called by some Thermopylae) and had driven him back from the entrance.[4]

§2 And so now he has made peace with the Athenians, passed without opposition within the Gates,[5] and destroyed the Phocian nation, and in the Amphictyonic Council he has received from the rest of the Greeks the territory of the Phocians and their votes on the council.[6] He has also sent envoys to the Athenians, claiming that they too should concede these points. Demosthenes advises the Athenians to make the acknowledgement, though he does not support the matter as being correct or proper, nor does he say that it is right that the

---

[1] That is, the war with Philip, declared in early 356.

[2] In the 8 years of the war, the only Athenian success was at Thermopylae in 352 (IV.17 and note, for refs). The response to D.'s *Olynthiacs* was poor, especially in terms of forces sent over and above those already stationed in the north— which were small enough (cf. Cawkwell, *CQ* 1962, 131-2).

[3] For his promise to settle the Phocian war in the Thessalians' interests, or on their behalf, cf. II.7 and note. However, if Philip made promises to Thebes (Cloché, for example, disagrees, *Thèbes de Béotie*, p. 180), we are ignorant of their terms. The ancient sources in general are not in agreement on Philip's intentions towards Thebes at this stage; compare, for example, Just. VIII.2 with DS XVI.58.2-4 and §§21-22, below. On the handing over to Thebes of Orchomenos and Koroneia, §§21-22, below, VI.13-15, DS XVI.58.

[4] IV.17 and note for refs. 'Driven', a fair translation of L.'s term, is too strong for what appears to have happened. There is not a suggestion elsewhere that the Athenian force did anything but block the pass (DS XVI.38.1-2; Just. VIII.2; Dem. XVIII.32).

[5] For the chronology of the period, cf. my Appendix, 'Chronological Table'.

[6] DS XVI.59-60; Just. VIII.4, 5; Dem. XIX.53-66, 325; Tod No. 172; for further refs, Beloch III.1.510-15.

The Spectre of Philip

Macedonians should have a part in a Greek council; instead, he claims that he is afraid that they may be compelled to take on a general war against all the Greeks.[7] For, he says, various states have been thrown into conflict with the Athenians for various reasons, and these will combine to make war on the Athenians, he says, 'if we give them this common pretext against us, namely that we alone oppose the decrees of the Amphictyons. Thus it is better for us to maintain the peace, since Philip has passed within the Gates and is able to march against Attica, than to take on so great a danger over a petty issue.'[8]

§3 It seems to me that this speech was prepared but not spoken. For when the orator is accusing Aeschines,[9] he makes this charge also against him, along with the other accusations, that Aeschines advised the Athenians to vote that Philip should become an Amphictyon, though nobody else dared to introduce the proposal, not even that most shameless of creatures, Philocrates.[10] Therefore if he himself had given advice on this situation, he would not be using it to attack Aeschines; but he was obviously afraid of the suspicion that he might appear to be siding with Philip and to be putting forward such an opinion because he had been trusted by the king. For even in the speech it is obvious that he is facing up to such suspicion when he tries to represent himself as being patriotic and incorruptible.[11]

---

[7] §§24-25 et passim, below.
[8] Not an exact quotation, at least from the extant text, but cf. §§14-19.
[9] In the speech *On the False Embassy*, delivered in 343.
[10] Ibid., 111-113.
[11] Blass, III.1.342-3, discusses this point, noting the difference between active advocacy of and merely not opposing the Amphictyons' request. While the former is plainly the charge against Aeschines, the latter is equally plainly D.'s intention in this speech (§§13, 14-19, 24-25). Blass also thinks that this speech was probably delivered later than the occasion mentioned above (note 10), on the grounds that it also contains issues of a more general nature than the specific question of Philip's admission to the council. The latter is certainly a part of the speech (§19), but is not treated as particularly more urgent than the general considerations of policy towards Philip, the Amphictyons and the other Greeks (cf. §§14-23). Blass may well be right; on the other hand, he assumes, perhaps wrongly, that Aeschines' speech was delivered at an assembly whose sole purpose was discussion of this one issue and that it was held *before* the meeting at which the present speech was delivered. Neither claim seems justified on the evidence, which is just not full enough to be sure.

TRANSLATION AND COMMENTARY
On the Peace—late 346

§1 I see, men of Athens, that our affairs at the present moment are occasioning considerable difficulty and confusion, not only because many things have been abandoned by us and because there is nothing profitable in speaking well of them, but also because, in the case of what remains,[1] there is no unanimity of opinion as to what is expedient, even on a single point, some thinking this way and others completely differently. §2 Now deliberation is naturally a vexatious and difficult matter, but you yourselves, men of Athens, have made it much more difficult. For whereas the rest of mankind are accustomed to indulge in deliberation *before* action, you do this *after* action.[2] The result of this, for as long as I can remember, has always been that the man who censures your mistakes is held in high repute and thought to be a clever speaker, but your interests and the matters on which you are deliberating pass you by. §3 Nevertheless, though this is the case, I have risen to speak because I think and I am firmly convinced that if you are willing to desist from shouting and quarrelling and to listen instead—as men who are deliberating over their city and affairs of such magnitude ought to listen—then I shall be able both to tell you about and to advise you as to the means whereby the present situation will be improved and whereby what has been abandoned will be saved.[3]

§4 I know full well, men of Athens, that it is most advantageous for a man, if he has the effrontery, to speak in your assembly about himself and about the proposals he himself has made. But I think this is such a vulgar and offensive practice that, even though I see its necessity,

---

[1] The Greek is indefinite in meaning here; 'what remains' may mean 'what possessions remain to us' or 'what is to come [i.e., the future]'.

[2] Cf. IV.40-41.

[3] At this point, according to Blass, III.1.343, ends the first of the two proems to this speech. He believes the first (§§1-3) to be a later addition, not in fact belonging to the speech as delivered. His argument is convincing: the themes of this first part—the perversity of the Athenians, who deliberate after and not before the event, and the recovery of what has been lost (to which D. never returns)—are certainly unrelated to the rest of the speech. The first proem, as Blass remarks, is more like another *Philippic*.

I shrink from following it. I do think, however, that you could form a better judgement on the things that I shall say now if you recall to mind a few of those said by me on former occasions. §5 For first of all, men of Athens, when Euboea was in a state of disturbance and certain people[4] were trying to persuade you to send help to Plutarchus and to take upon yourselves an inglorious and costly war, I was the first—indeed the only one—to come forward and oppose the idea; and I was all but torn apart by those who for petty gains had persuaded you to make many gross mistakes. A short time passed by, and not only did you incur disgrace and suffer as no others of mankind have ever suffered at the hands of those to whom they had sent aid,[5] but you also all recognized both the wickedness of those who had persuaded you to such a course of action on that occasion and the excellence of my own advice.

§6 Again, men of Athens, I saw that the actor Neoptolemus[6] received safe conduct on the grounds of his profession, but was doing the greatest harm to the city and was managing and manipulating in Philip's interests the commissions he received from you. Accordingly, I came forward and addressed you—and I was not motivated by any personal enmity or desire to lay a false accusation, as has become plain from subsequent events. §7 And in this affair I shall no longer blame those who spoke on Neoptolemus' behalf—to be sure, there was nobody at all who *did* speak on his behalf—but you yourselves. For if you had been watching the tragedies in the theatre of Dionysus instead of being engaged in a debate dealing with your security and matters affecting the whole State,[7] you could not have given such a partial hearing to Neoptolemus or such a hostile one to myself. §8 And yet this at least

---

[4] Among the 'certain people' referred to there is certainly Eubulus, supported by Meidias, who urged the Athenian aid to Euboea (*see* note 5, below). It is noteworthy that Athenian citizens are not normally criticized by name in the assembly (cf. also §10 below, etc.); the same does not apply however to non-citizens or ex-citizens (e.g., Neoptolemus, §§6-8; Callias, II.19).

[5] This was the Euboean campaign of early 348 (Cawkwell, *CQ* 1962, 127-30). Our main source is Plutarch *Phocion* XII-XIV; cf. also Aes. III.86-88, II.12, 169, Dem. XXIII.132-135, 161-168, XXXIX.16-17; Parke, *JHS* 1929, 246-52 (but also Cawkwell, *CQ*, 127-30).

[6] Neoptolemus, born in Skyros (schol. Dem. V.6, Ddf. p. 161, *ll*. 21-27), was a tragic actor and earned acclaim thereby at Pella. He was among those who advised Athens of Philip's willingness to negotiate for peace (XIX.315), for which he was later attacked by D. (XIX.12, 315). Cf. also DS XVI.92-93, Suet. *Cal.* 57, Plut. *Mor.* 844F. The immunity of the actor was probably not formally guaranteed, but as a professional entertainer (who, in addition, could lay claim to a religious function), he aroused no suspicion by travelling from festival to festival in pursuit of his livelihood.

[7] That is, the debate preceding the dispatch of the first embassy to Macedon, in February 346 (XIX.12ff.).

Translation and Commentary: On the Peace — late 346

I think you have all realized by now, that although Neoptolemus left Athens at that time to go to the enemy's country in order, so he claimed, to recover monies owing to him in Macedonia so that he could perform his liturgies here;[8] and although he made great play with the argument that it was a terrible thing to level accusations at those who were transferring their wealth from Macedonia to Athens; yet, as soon as the Peace had guaranteed his security, he liquidated all the real estate he possessed here and took himself and his cash off to Philip. §9 These, then, are two cases of warnings that I gave you in advance. They are testimonies for the speeches I have made, since they were disclosed by me with accuracy and correctness, exactly as they were.

A third case, men of Athens, and I shall just mention this one thing and then say what I have come forward to say—a third case was when we ambassadors had returned to Athens after receiving from Philip the oaths concerning the Peace.[9] §10 Certain people were then promising that Thespiae and Plataea would be re-populated, that if Philip gained control he would preserve the Phocians but break up Thebes into villages, that Oropus would be ours and that Euboea would be restored to us in return for Amphipolis.[10] Led on by such hopes and chicaneries as these, you have abandoned the Phocians in a way that is neither in your interests nor perhaps honourable. But it will be obvious to you that I neither deceived you nor kept quiet about these things, but forewarned you, as I am sure you recollect, that I neither had knowledge of such things nor any anticipation of their happening, and that I thought the person who said all this was babbling nonsense.[11]

[8] On the performance of liturgies, IV.36 and notes.

[9] The return of this, the second embassy, was on 13 *Skirophorion* (7 July?) 346, the deliberations in the council taking place on the 15th, in the assembly on the 16th (*see* my Appendix, 'Chronological Table').

[10] On the term 'certain persons', §5 and note, above. These promises, D. claims elsewhere, were made on Philip's behalf but without his authority by Aeschines and Philocrates (compare VI.28-30 with XIX.41-46). Aeschines' motive in making them can only be conjectured: whether he thought the end justified the means, whether he was over-zealous in interpreting Philip's good will towards Athens, or whether he was paid by Philip to mislead the Athenians. Cf. VI.28-30, XIX.41-46, 158-161, 166-168, etc. In any case D. has grossly distorted the facts here. Athens had no option but to 'abandon the Phocians' because Philip was within close striking distance of Thermopylae when he signed the agreement for the Peace; cf. Aes. III.130-135, Dem. XIX.34, 58; Sealey, WS 1966, 145-52.

[11] 'The person' (cf. §5 and note) was Aeschines (cf. for example, XIX.8, 19-24). As noted above, we cannot tell Aeschines' motive in putting forward this 'babbling nonsense'; at least, we may safely discount the possibility that he was betraying Athens; apart from D.'s worst slanders there is no evidence to show that he ever acted in a way inconsistent with what he thought best for Athens. For Aeschines' part in *Skirophorion* 346, cf. Cawkwell, *REG* 1962.

The Spectre of Philip

§11 I shall not refer, men of Athens, to any special cleverness or boastful pretension in all these cases where I obviously have better foresight than the rest, nor shall I claim to get to know and perceive them in advance through any other means than those which I shall tell you. They are two in number: one, men of Athens, is good fortune, which I see is stronger than all the cleverness and wisdom that exists in mankind; §12 the second is the fact that my judgement and calculation of affairs of State are not affected by vested interests, and nobody could point to any financial gain attached to my political acts and speeches. Therefore, any advantage that might be gained from the actual political circumstances is seen by me in an undistorted light. But whenever you add money to one pan, as it were, of the scales, it carries away and drags down the reasoning powers with it; and once a man has done this, he can no longer reason accurately and soundly about anything.[12]

§13 One thing, then, I maintain to be an essential prerequisite if one wishes to secure allies or contributions[13] or anything else for the city: he must do it without breaking the existing peace; not on the ground that it is a marvellous peace nor that it is worthy of you; but whatever sort of peace it is, it would have been more in our interest that it had never been made than for it to be broken by us now that it has been made. For we have cast away many advantages which we possessed when we made the peace; so that war would have been safer and easier then than it would be now.[14] §14 Secondly, we must see to it, men of Athens, that we do not move these men who have come together and claim to be Amphictyons to the necessity or the excuse of a joint war against us. For, in my opinion, if we should again become embroiled in war with Philip on account of Amphipolis[15] or some such claim of our own, in which the Thessalians, the Argives and the Thebans have no part, I do not think that any of these people would make war on us, §15 least of all the Thebans. (And please let no one shout me down until he has heard what I have to say.) I think this not because the Thebans have any affection for us, nor because they would not gratify Philip, but they are well aware, even though one asserts that they are totally devoid of intelligence,[16] that if they become involved in a war

---

[12] Cf. Pericles' speech, Thuc. II.60ff.

[13] 'Contribution' (*syntaxis*) was the euphemistic equivalent in the Second Athenian League of the tribute (*phoros*) of the fifth-century empire (Marshall, pp. 38-42; but *see also* Marshall, Appendix, p. 130).

[14] Athens' primary disadvantages now are two: Philip has control of Thermopylae and Athens has lost the (doubtful) allegiance of the Phocians, who have been utterly crushed.

[15] Cf. §25 and note 16, below.

[16] This seems to have been the general Athenian opinion of Thebans, or of Boeotians in general; cf. XVIII.43; Plat. *Phaedo* 64B; also Pindar *Ol.* VI.90.

against us, they will have all the evils of war while another sits on the sidelines waiting for the benefits. They will not, therefore, let themselves in for this unless the origin and the cause of the war concerns all alike.[17] §16 Nor again do I think that we would come to grief if we were to make war on the Thebans over Oropus or some such private dispute.[18] For I think that those who would help us or the Thebans would send their aid in the event of an invasion being made into their ally's own country, but they would not join with either side in a campaign of aggression. §17 Indeed, alliances worth considering have this characteristic and things naturally work out like this. Our respective allies are not so well disposed towards us or the Thebans as to desire in equal measure that we be secure and that we obtain supremacy over the other states; rather all of them might well desire our security for their own sake, but not one of them would wish either side to gain supremacy and so become their own masters.

What then do I consider to be dangerous and what, in my opinion, must we guard against? We must be careful that the coming war[19] shall not furnish all alike with a common pretext and a common ground of complaint against us. §18 For if the Argives and the Messenians and the Megalopolitans and certain of the other Peloponnesians, whose sympathies are with them, shall be hostile towards us because of our peace negotiations with the Spartans and because they think that we are giving our approval to certain of Sparta's policies;[20] and if the

[17] Compare with I.26 and note.
[18] Oropus had long been a subject of dispute. A town on the Athenian side of the Attic/Boeotian border, it was seized by the Boeotians in 412 BC (Thuc. VIII.60) and again in 402 (DS XIV.17.1-3). In the 370s it was still disputed (Isoc. XIV.20, 37). In 366 it was seized by exiles aided by Themison of Eretria and handed over to Thebes, after which bitter dispute over it continued (DS XV.76.1; Xen. HG VII.4.1; Dem. XVIII.99; Aes. II.164, III.85). In 353 Sparta asserted that it should be restored to Athens, but nothing came of this (Dem. XVI.4, 16, and §24, below).
[19] Although the Greek participial adjective *mellon* may be so translated, it seems unlikely that the Loeb rendering (*Demosthenes*, Vol. I, p. 113), 'the *inevitable* war', is what D. intends; the force of his warnings against provoking the Amphictyons is lost thereby. Taken as 'the *coming* war', it probably refers simply to the future possibility of a private war against Thebes over Oropus (§16), or against Macedon over Amphipolis (§14), etc. This translation appears to be more consistent with the theme of the speech: if D. is heeded, there is no 'inevitable' war. Athens must avoid war except on the possible (and future) occasions on which only one opponent need be involved.
[20] In Speech XVI (*For the Megalopolitans*) *passim*, D. argued that Messene, Megalopolis and Arcadia must not be abandoned to Sparta. These and other neighbours of Sparta have every reason to fear her imperialistic ventures and to suspect Athenian motives should they decide to seek Spartan aid—which would certainly involve reciprocal agreements (ibid. 16-18).

The Spectre of Philip

Thebans, who are already, so they say, inimical towards us, shall become even more so because we are harbouring their exiles and are displaying towards them in every possible way our ill-will; §19 and if the Thessalians shall be against us because we are harbouring the Phocian exiles, and Philip because we are stopping him from participating in the Delphic Amphictyony; then I am afraid that, each group having its own private cause for resentment, they may conduct the war against us in concert, putting forward as a pretext the decrees of the Amphictyons, and may each then be lured on beyond their own individual interests, as also happened in the case of the Phocians.[21]

§20 For you realize, I suppose, that the Thebans, Philip and the Thessalians just now acted in accord, though each of them had completely different aims. For example, the Thebans were unable to prevent Philip from passing through Thermopylae and seizing the passes,[22] nor could they stop him from coming on the scene at the last moment[23] and winning the glory for all that they themselves had been toiling over. §21 For although the Thebans have now had some success as regards the recovery of their territory, as far as honour and glory are concerned they have come off most shamefully. For it appears that they would have gained nothing had Philip not passed through Thermopylae. This the Thebans did not want; but they put up with all this because they wanted to seize Orchomenos and Koroneia but could not otherwise do so. §22 Some people indeed actually have the temerity to say that Philip did not want to hand over Orchomenos and Koroneia, but was forced to.[24] Though I wish these men well of their opinions, I do know that Philip's concern for these places was no stronger than his desire to seize the passes and to gain the glory of appearing to have put an end to the war by himself and to manage the Pythian games all by himself. These were the objects he was striving after above all. §23 The Thessalians, for their part, desired neither of these two—either the Thebans or Philip—to grow powerful (for they thought that either event was a threat to themselves). They did desire to gain control of the Amphictyonic Council[25] and affairs at Delphi—two distinct gains

---

[21] Cf. Just. VIII.1 and DS XVI.23 for the Theban use of the Amphictyonic Council for her own ends. The result of course is not what anyone might have expected; none of the Amphictyons has gained exactly what it wanted (Libanius' Introduction to Speech V.2, §§20-23, below).

[22] July 346; cf. my Appendix, 'Chronological Table'.

[23] That is, to put an end to the Sacred War; cf. VIII.63.

[24] Libanius' Introduction to Speech V.1 and note.

[25] Cf. II.7, 11, I.22 and notes. The Thessalian League was numerically the major power in the Amphictyonic Council, controlling or influencing more than half of the votes (Westlake, p. 98). It seems unlikely that the Thessalians played a major role in the fomenting of the Sacred War (although a Thessalian

for them. And because they aimed at these they joined with Philip in the acts I have mentioned. So you will find that each party was led on by its own private ambitions to do much that it did not want to do. This, however, this is what we must guard against.

§24 'Must we then do Philip's bidding for fear of these things? Is that what you of all people are telling us to do?' Far from it. But I do think that we should act so that we neither do anything unworthy of ourselves nor become involved in war, so that we shall give everyone the impression that we have common sense and are making just claims. To those who boldly think that we ought to endure anything and everything and who do not foresee the war that will follow, I wish to put forward the following considerations. We are permitting the Thebans to hold Oropus,[26] and if anyone, after telling us to give a straightforward answer, should ask us why, we would say, 'So that we do not go to war with them'. §25 Again, we have now given up Amphipolis to Philip, in accordance with the treaty,[27] and we allow the people of Cardia to occupy a position apart from the rest of the inhabitants of the Chersonese:[28] and we permit the Carian to seize the islands of Chios, Cos and Rhodes[29] and the Byzantines to beach our merchant-vessels,[30] obviously because we think that the tranquillity coming from peace brings more benefits than clashing and quarrelling over these points. It is foolish therefore and utterly irresponsible, when

---

proposed the decree banishing the pro-Phocian party from Delphi in 363; H&H No. 116, *l.* 16); they already faced the tyrants of Pherae and would hardly have welcomed a war on a new front (Westlake, p. 169). However once Delphi was seized (DS XVI.24), the threat to the Thessalian dominance was obvious and the League would certainly risk much to remove it (Just. VIII.4.5).

[26] §16 and note, above.

[27] Under the Peace of Philocrates, the possessions of the contracting parties held at the time of the ratification of the Peace were to be retained by them (Ps-Dem. VII.18, XII.8-11).

[28] Ps-Dem. VII.39-45, VIII.64, XII.11, XIX.174.

[29] Cf. XV.3-4. The Carian is Idreus, satrap of Caria from 350 to 344 and brother of Mausolus, who had aided the revolt of Chios, Cos and Rhodes from Athens in the Social War, 357-5. Our knowledge of Idreus is slight, but we do know that Miletus dedicated to Apollo, in Delphi, statues of him and his wife (Homolle, *BCH* 1899, 385ff.). Isocrates considered him a likely ally for Greece in a war against Persia (*Philippus* 103-104). However, Idreus remained loyal to Persia (DS XVI.42, 46.1; Beloch III.2.285-7; *CAH* VI.152-3; but cf. Cawkwell, *CQ* 1963, 136-8 for dating). Cf. also Dem. XV *passim*.

[30] The Byzantines, now no longer members of the Athenian League but in alliance with Philip (IV.6 and note; Marshall, pp. 109, 113), are apparently insisting that the Athenian corn-ships land and sell their cargo to Byzantium, a common practice in times of corn-shortage in the fourth century (cf. for example, [Arist.] *Econ.* II.30, 1346b).

The Spectre of Philip

we have behaved thus towards each of our enemies individually, concerning our personal and most important affairs, that we should now go to war against all of them together over the shadow at Delphi.[31]

---

[31] An adaptation of the saying 'to fight for an ass's shadow' (Ar. *Wasps*, l. 191, Plat. *Phaedrus* 260C), to fight for a trifling cause. D. means that neither the importance of the Amphictyonic Council itself nor the honour of membership of it is sufficient to justify going to war—presumably, that is, after Philip's admission to and virtual control of it has cheapened it.

APPENDIXES

THE THEORIKON

The different aspects of the question of the Theoric Fund have been widely discussed with, until recently, markedly little success. The only study that reconciles all the available evidence is that by Cawkwell, in the course of his article on Eubulus, *JHS* 1963, esp. 53-61. It should suffice, in general, to consult this article, but a few points that have caused much confusion in the past should be stressed here.

Most scholars agree that the amount of the theoric *distribution* was 'very small beer' (Jones, pp. 33-4, who estimates a total payment of 15 talents per year, high rather than low in comparison with other estimates). This makes nonsense (as he concedes, pp. 33-4) of the efforts made by Demosthenes to have the law or laws governing the distribution repealed. Why risk the overthrow of his whole scheme by proposing an extremely unpopular measure that would increase the military finance by so little as to be scarcely worth while? The only answer that makes sense of the facts we have is that the Theoric Commission formed by Eubulus somewhere between 355 and 353/2 controlled much more money than was actually distributed as festival-dole (Cawkwell, *JHS* 1963, 55-8). It is possible that to this money the control of the festival-dole was added by Eubulus, in order to give the populace good reason for opposing any change to the theoric laws.

Among others, Jones (p. 33) cites Dem. LIX.4-5, which states that the theoric monies were transferred by law to the *stratiotikon* (military fund) in time of war. But this is plainly unacceptable; Athens, at the time of the *Olynthiacs*, had been at war with Philip for 8 years, yet Demosthenes was pressing for what the speaker of Dem. LIX claims already existed. Cawkwell (*JHS* 1963, 58-61) makes the speaker refer to the time before Eubulus' theoric law, which seems to have actually forbidden the use of these monies for military purposes, whatever the circumstances. Obviously, Eubulus' aim in this was to prevent the

The Spectre of Philip

making of rash decisions to commit troops and money to unnecessary objectives, or indeed to any objectives, when the finances of Athens after the Social War were so low.

Thus, the system may be reconstructed as follows. Before 355, there was a fund in existence which provided the poorer people with festival-dole; in time of war, the monies it controlled reverted automatically to the *stratiotikon*. Between 355 and 353/2, Eubulus passed a law or laws which (a) tied up the excess money above State expenditure for peaceful use, forbidding the previously automatic transfer to the *stratiotikon* in time of war. To attempt a reversion to the previous system was to incur the risk of *graphe paranomon* (indictment for making unconstitutional proposals). However, as this charge was decided by a normal jury, the law(s) provided the additional safeguard (b) that the distribution of festival-dole was tied to the Theoric Commission's control of the other theoric monies. So as well as being a contraversion of the law, to transfer the *theorikon* to the *stratiotikon* was to lose the festival-dole as well to military use.

Demosthenes' hesitation in broaching the subject was the result of the double deterrent: he would incur the risk both of the anger of the poorer citizens and of the charge of *graphe paranomon*.

However, in February 348, when Athens' resources were strained beyond their limits (XXXIX.17) by the needs of the Euboean expedition, Apollodorus proposed to the people that they decide whether the excess over State expenditure be used for military purposes (LIX.4). There ensued, according to the speaker of LIX, a unanimous vote to this end (XXXIX.5), but Apollodorus was subsequently indicted for his proposal and fined 15 talents (XXXIX.6).

At some time, presumably shortly afterwards, according to an unreliable source (who might nevertheless be right; schol. Dem.I.1, Ddf., p. 33, *ll.* 11-15; Cawkwell, *JHS* 1963, 59-61), Eubulus passed a law imposing the death-penalty on anyone who attempted to emulate Apollodorus. (While I concede that this particular scholiastic statement is doubtful, because of its context (Cawkwell, *JHS* 1963, 59-61), I cannot follow Cawkwell's objection to this point; there seems to me no inconsistency in assuming (a) that between 355 and 348, the deterrent to people like Demosthenes and Apollodorus was the process of *graphe paranomon*, under which the latter was fined, and (b) that once Apollodorus' attempt had been at least initially successful, Eubulus or someone else might have felt that a further deterrent was necessary.)

At any rate, eventually the laws were revised, probably in the first days of 339/8 (Cawkwell, *JHS* 1963, 61), and Demosthenes was able to move successfully that the money in question be transferred to the *stratiotikon*. It had taken Philip's attack on the Hellespont and his

The Theorikon

march into central Greece to induce the Athenians to succumb to Demosthenes' pressure.

For further details cf. Cawkwell, *JHS* 1963, 61, and the refs cited at Libanius' Introduction to *Olynthiacs* I, note 18. A more detailed treatment of the Theorikon, as well as other forms of monetary distribution, may be found in Buchanan, *Theorika* especially pp. 28-88.

SELECTION OF HISTORICAL FRAGMENTS
PHILOCHORUS OF ATHENS
(Jacoby, *FGH* IIIB, No. 328)

F 33

(Harpokration *under 'theorika'*)
Demosthenes in his speech against Philip (III.11, 31 ?). Theoric monies were certain funds in the public Treasury collected from the revenues of the city. These monies were originally preserved for the needs of war and were called 'stratiotic' funds. Later they were paid out on public works and distributions to the citizens; the demagogue Agyrrhios was the first to begin these distributions. Philochorus in Book III of his *Atthis* says: 'the theoric money was at first reckoned as a drachma[1] for a seat in the theatre at the dramatic festivals and it was from this that it got its name',[2] and so on.

F 41

(Harpokration *under 'symmoria'*)
Demosthenes in his first speech against Aphobus (XXVII.7). At Athens, unlike the practice among us, it was not the whole populace divided among the symmories, but only the wealthy who were able to pay the property-tax to the city. . . . The Athenians were first divided into symmories in the archonship of Nausinikos (378/7), as Philochorus says in the fifth book of the *Atthis*.

F 49-51

(D.Hal. *ep. ad Amm.* I.9)
This war (the Olynthian) took place in the archonship of Kallimachos, as Philochorus shows in the sixth book of his *Atthis*, where he writes

---

[1] In fact the theoric money to pay for a seat in the theatre was probably first distributed in the 440s (Jacoby IIIB Suppl. I.329), when the amount was 2 obols. In 395/4, 'in the archonship of Diophantos the theoric money became a drachma' (Zenobius *Paroemiographus* III.37), probably at the instigation of Agyrrhios.

[2] The Greek *theorikon* is the adjective from the noun *theoria* ('public spectacle at the theatre or games'). Philochorus says that *theorika* are monies given to purchase a *thea*, a seat in the theatre.

word for word as follows: 'Kallimachos of the deme Pergase. In his year of office (349/8) the Athenians made an alliance with the Olynthians, who were being attacked by Philip and had sent ambassadors to Athens ... and they sent aid to them consisting of 2,000 peltasts, the 30 triremes that were with Chares and 8 triremes which they manned in addition to these.' (50) Next, after describing the few intervening affairs, he proceeds thus: 'About the same time the Chalcidians on the Thracian coast were being hard-pressed by the war and so they sent an embassy to Athens. The Athenians dispatched to them Charidemus, the commander at the Hellespont. Charidemus, supported by the Olynthians and with 18 triremes, 4,000 peltasts and 150 cavalry, moved against Pallene and Bottiaia and ravaged the country.' (51) Then he speaks as follows about the third expeditionary force: 'When the Olynthians had again sent ambassadors to Athens and were begging the Athenians not to stand by and see them reduced by the war but to send, in addition to the troops already at Olynthus, an expeditionary force composed not of mercenaries but of Athenian citizens, the people sent them another 17 triremes and, from the citizen-body, 2,000 hoplites and 300 cavalry conveyed in transport-vessels. Chares was in command of the whole expedition.'

F 155

(Didymus *in Demosth.* XIII.7, col.13.42)

(Demosthenes) makes mention of the action adopted by the Athenians towards the Megarians concerning the holy meadow-land (III.20, XIII.32). This took place in the archonship of Apollodorus (350/49), as Philochorus relates when he writes as follows: 'The Athenians, having quarrelled with the Megarians over the boundaries of the holy meadow-land, went against Megara with Ephialtes, who was general for the home territory,[3] and had the boundaries of the holy meadow-land marked out. The men who marked out the boundaries, after the Megarians had agreed to this, were Lacratides the hierophant[4] and Hieroclides the torchbearer. They also established as sacred the estates bordering on the holy meadow-land, since the god had given the reply (i.e., to the commission sent to Delphi) that it would be more fitting and better if they left them alone and did not work them. They marked

---

[3] On the growth of specialized functions within the *strategia* see Daremberg and Saglio (V.2.1528). The Arist. *Ath.Pol.* (61.1) mentions 5 special generalships, as opposed to the other 5 which were concerned with matters of the moment. This Ephialtes is probably the same who in 340 went to Persia as ambassador and whose extradition was demanded by Alexander in 335 after the destruction of Thebes (Plut. *Mor.* 847F, 848E; Arr. I.10.4; Plut. *Dem.* XXIII).

[4] 'hierophant': the priest who conducted the initiating rites at Eleusis.

off the boundaries all around with stone pillars, according to the degree of Philocrates.'[5]

ANDROTION OF ATHENS
(Jacoby IIIB, No. 324)

F 30

(Didymus *in Demosth*. XIII.7, col.13.42)

(Demosthenes at XIII.32, III.20) makes mention of the action adopted by the Athenians towards the Megarians concerning the holy meadow-land. This took place in the archonship of Apollodorus (350/49), as Philochorus relates when he writes as follows: . . . (cf. Philochorus F 155) . . . Andretion has also discussed this holy meadow-land in Book VII of his *Atthis*. He writes as follows: 'The Athenians defined, with reference to the Megarians, the boundaries of the holy meadow-land of the Twin Goddesses, how they wished them to be defined.[6] For the Megarians agreed that the hierophant Lacratides and the torch-bearer Hieroclides should be the definers of the boundaries. And when they had marked out the boundaries they abode by them. They also

---

[5] Probably Philocrates of the deme Hagnos, the author of the Peace of 346, who, a follower of Eubulus, most likely was already playing a prominent role in the 350s. The background of this affair (on which cf. also Androtion F 30) is preserved in *IG* II² 204, dated 352/1. By this decree an Athenian board was established 'to give judgement in the temple of Demeter in the city concerning the disputed boundaries of the holy meadow-land' (*ll*. 7-8). A commission of 3 was sent to Delphi to consult Apollo on the question 'whether it is more fitting and better for the people of Athens that the king-archon lease out those parts of the holy meadow-land within the boundaries which have been put under cultivation . . .' or whether these areas 'should be left alone, dedicated to the Twin Goddesses' (*ll*. 25-30). Perhaps Eubulus wished to exploit the land commercially (Glotz and Cohen III.246, 279; Jacoby IIIB Suppl. 1.425). During the marking-out differences occurred with the Megarians, perhaps, if we accept Jacoby's account, because the latter felt that the Athenians were illegally trying to extend the boundaries. A decree was passed 'to march out against the accursed Megarians' (Dem. XIII.32), probably during the year 351/0 (Jacoby IIIB Suppl. 1.425), but operations did not begin until the following year, the archonship of Apollodorus, as F 155 states. The Megarians were compelled to back down and the demarcation was left to Lacratides and Hieroclides. Corinth, presumably in support of Megara in this affair, omitted Athens from those invited to the biennial Isthmian Games (Aristid. *Panath*. i 311), perhaps those of spring 350. However an Athenian military demonstration was sufficient to convince the Corinthians of their error; the invitation was duly issued. It is worth noting the legacy of anti-Athenian feeling left at least partly as a result of these disputes; 6 years afterwards, in 343, Philip was able to win sympathy and support without difficulty in Megara (especially) and Corinth (IX.17-18, XIX.87, 204, 294-295, 326, 334, XVIII.71, 295).

[6] The Greek is ambiguous as to the meaning of the 'they'; the Athenians, the Megarians or the Twin Goddesses? The last appears most likely; they would indicate their wishes through the Oracle at Delphi.

dedicated all the estates adjacent to the holy meadow-land, since, when they consulted the Oracle, the god had replied that it would be more fitting and better if they did not work them. The boundary was marked out all around with stone pillars on the motion of Philocrates.'

ANAXIMENES OF LAMPSACUS
(Jacoby IIA, No. 72)

F 4

(Harpokration and Suda *under 'Pezetairoi'*)

Demosthenes in his orations against Philip (II.17). Anaximenes, in the first book of his *Philippic Histories*, when talking about Alexander says: 'Next, after making the most renowned men accustomed to serving as cavalry, he called them "Companions";[7] the majority and those who served on foot he divided into companies, platoons[8] and other commands and named them *pezetairoi* (foot-companions). He did this so that both sections might participate in the royal companionship and thus be continually very zealous in their loyalty towards him.'

THEOPOMPUS OF CHIOS
(Jacoby IIB, No. 115)

F 30

(a) (Harpokration *Epit. Suda*)

What is the meaning of the phrase found in the *Philippics* of Demosthenes (II.6) 'that notorious secret'? Theopompus, in Book I of his *Philippic Histories*, has shown us. For he says: 'And (the Athenian people) sent to Philip Antiphon and Charidemus as ambassadors to negotiate with him about friendship. When these two had reached Philip they tried to persuade him in secret to co-operate with the Athenians so that they might take Amphipolis; to Philip they promised Pydna. The Athenian ambassadors made no report of this to the people, since they wished to conceal from the people of Pydna that they were going to betray them; instead they dealt in secret with the Council of 500.'

(b) (Schol. Dem. II.6, Ddf. p. 85, *l*. 19)

Why 'in secret'? In order that both parties—the Potidaeans and the Pydnaeans—might not find out and take precautions. Theopompus says that the business concerned only Pydna and Philip, in order that

---

[7] On the Companion cavalry (as compared with the Companions of the King) cf. Tarn II.138ff., 154ff.; and Berve I.104ff. In general on this fragment cf. note to II.17 and refs cited there.

[8] *dekas*: literally a file of 10 men. By the end of Alexander's reign the *dekas* had grown to 16 (Arr. VII.23).

The Spectre of Philip

Philip might give Amphipolis to the Athenians and receive from them Pydna, which was his own possession. And the secret negotiations were in order that the Pydnaeans might not learn about them and take precautions. For they did not want to be subjected to Philip.

F 81
(Athenaeus VI.76, 259F–260A)

Indeed Theopompus also in Book IX of his *Philippic History* says: 'Agathocles, although he had been a slave and one of the *penestai*[9] from Thessaly, had great influence with Philip because of his flattery and because he used to dance and create merriment when in Philip's company at drinking-parties. Because of this influence Philip sent him to corrupt the Perrhaebaeans[10] and to look after affairs in that area. Such was the sort of rogue the Macedonian always had around him. He used in general to spend more time with these because of their fondness for drink and their scurrilous humour; and when he was deliberating on matters of the highest moment he would make use of them for counsellors.'

F 99
(Harpokration *under* 'Euboulos')

Theopompus in Book X of his *Philippic History* states that Eubulus was a most renowned leader of the people, a man of thrift and industry and a man who provided much money and distributed it to the Athenians; this was why it came about that during his political life the city became most unmanly and idle.[11]

F 127
(Theon *Progymnasmata* 2)

... and as examples of the story used to illustrate a point there is the sort we find in Herodotus about the flute-player (I.141) and in Philistus about the horse (F 6, Jacoby No. 555) ... and in the twentieth book of Theopompus' *Philippic History* is the story about War and Arrogance, which Philip relates to the leaders of the Chalcidians.[12]

---

[9] *penestai*: Thessalian serfs, equivalent to the Laconian helots, a conquered tribe originally but later expanded by the addition of prisoners-of-war, etc. Cf. OCD and *under* 'Serfs'.

[10] 'Perrhaebaea': of strategic importance, especially because of its city of Gonnos (Hdt. VII.128), which commanded the entrance to the Vale of Tempe. Agathocles' task was presumably that of subverting the support of the anti-Macedonian faction (hence 'corrupt') in order to secure the pass for Philip.

[11] A typically censorious judgement by Theopompus and one which takes into account none of the external factors influencing Athens at this time.

[12] The story of War and Arrogance is told by the fabulist Babrius (*Fable* 70): 'When the gods were being married, as each was being joined with his partner,

Selection of Historical Fragments

F 224

(Athenaeus IV.62, 166F-167C)

In the forty-ninth book of his *Histories* Theopompus writes as follows about the profligacy and way of life of Philip and his Companions: 'When Philip had become master of a large amount of money he did not spend it rapidly; rather he tossed it out and threw it away, for he was the worst administrator in the world. The members of his court too were just like him. For, in a word, not one of them knew how to live an honest life or even to manage a household with prudence. Philip himself was to blame for this, since he was insatiable and a spendthrift and did everything in a hurry, whether getting or giving. For because he was a soldier he had so little spare time that he was unable to reckon up his income and expenditure. Furthermore, his Companions were men who had gathered together from many regions—some from Macedonia itself, others from Thessaly and others from the rest of Greece. They were not selected on the basis of excellence; rather almost all the men of a lewd, disgusting or arrogant way of life from among both the Greeks and the barbarians gathered in Macedonia and were given the title "Companions of Philip". If anyone went there who was not this sort of person he rapidly became like them under the influence of the Macedonian way of life and manners. For they were impelled to be rogues and to live not in an orderly fashion but prodigally and like bandits, partly by the wars and campaigns and partly by the extravagances of Macedonian life.'

F 225

(a) (Polybius VIII.9.5ff.)

If anyone should wish to read the beginning of the forty-ninth book (of Theopompus' *Philippic History*) he would be absolutely amazed at the absurdity of the historian. For apart from anything else he has dared to write even the following (and I have set down the actual words he used): 'For almost all the men of a lewd or arrogant way of life from among both the Greeks and the barbarians gathered in

---

War was present on every occasion, since his was the last lot to be drawn. He married Arrogance, who alone was left for him to take; and with her, so the story goes, he fell deeply in love and he follows her wherever she goes. May Arrogance never come upon the cities of men, smiling on their peoples, for hot on her heels will come War.' Jacoby (IIB Kommentar, 378) dates the references in the remaining fragments (125-127) of Book XX to the year 351/0. F 125 refers to a Thracian town, F 126 to a Macedonian district on the Thracian border and F 127 to the Chalcidians. Whether we are to assume that Philip simply warned the Chalcidians with an improving story or that he showed more concrete disapproval of Olynthian overtures to Athens (Dem. I.13, IV.17 and notes) is a matter of conjecture.

The Spectre of Philip

Macedonia at Philip's court and were given the title "Companions of the King". For in general Philip used to reject those who were orderly in their habits and who looked after their personal property, but he would hold in honour and promote those who were spendthrifts and who spent their lives amid drinking and dicing. Therefore he not only accustomed them to have these habits but he also made them trained practitioners of every other kind of wickedness and beastliness. For what that is shameful or dreadful was not part of their character? Or what that is honourable and worth while was not absent from their character? Some of them continually shaved and smoothed off their bodies, even though they were men, and others had the audacity to mount each other, even though they had beards. They used to take around with them two or three men to make love to and they would even themselves provide for others the same services as these minions. Hence one would with justice regard them not as courtiers but as courtesans and would call them not soldiers but sodomites.[13] For whereas they were slayers of men by nature, by their way of life they were male prostitutes. To put the matter in a nutshell', he says, 'and in order not to go on at too great a length, especially since so many other matters surround me like a deluge, I think that those who were called "Friends and Companions of Philip" were more brutish and bestial in their disposition than either the Centaurs who dwelt on Pelion or the Laestrygonians who inhabited the plain of Leontine or any others you can think of.'

(b) (Athenaeus VI.77, 260D-261A)

'... and in addition to all this[14] they loved to be drunk instead of sober and they desired to loot and murder instead of living with moderation. They thought that telling the truth and abiding by their agreements did not concern them, but they considered perjury and cheating to be among the things most worthy of reverence. They neglected what they had and coveted what they did not have—and that even though they possessed no small part of Europe. For I think that although the Com-

[13] There are two puns here: *hetairos* ('companion', translated here as 'courtier') and *hetaira* ('courtesan'); *androphonoi* ('slayers of men', translated as 'soldiers') and *andropornoi* ('sodomites', 'male prostitutes'). On the question of affectation amongst Philip's followers many anecdotes are preserved in other sources, many of them obviously contradictory to those of Theopompus. One example (Plut. *Mor.* 178F) claims that Philip appointed one of Antipater's friends to the judiciary, but later, on learning that the man dyed his beard and hair, he discharged him on the grounds that a man who was untrustworthy in the matter of hair was not likely to be trustworthy in his actions.

[14] The early part of this fragment Athenaeus quotes in almost the same words as does Polybius. The translation given here begins from near the end of 225a, after '... by their way of life they were male prostitutes'.

Selection of Historical Fragments

panions at that time numbered no more than 800, they enjoyed the revenues of no less land than 10,000 of the richest Greeks with the most land.'

F 236
(Athenaeus X.46, 435BC)
In the fifty-third book, after he has spoken about the events at Chaeronea and after he has related how (Philip) invited to dinner the Athenian ambassadors who had come to him, he says: 'When (the Athenian ambassadors) had withdrawn, Philip immediately sent for certain of his Companions and bade them summon the flute-girls, the harpist Aristonicus, the flute-player Doron and all the others who were accustomed to drink with him. For Philip used to take such people around with him everywhere and he had equipped himself with many of the things that were used in drinking-sessions and parties. For being a man who was fond of drink and was of an incontinent temperament, he used to have about him many coarse buffoons and many who were of a musical inclination or of a ready wit. When he had drunk the whole night through, had made himself deeply intoxicated and had made much sport, he allowed all the rest of the company to depart while he (and it was now almost dawn) began to make his way in drunken revelry towards the Athenian ambassadors.'[15]

---

[15] With this fragment compare also F 163 (Athenaeus X.46, 435A): 'Philip, the father of Alexander, was also fond of drink, as Theopompus narrates in Book XXVI of his *Histories*', and F 282 (ibid., 435B) . . . and in another part of his *History* he writes: 'Philip was a madman and impetuous when faced with dangers; this was partly the result of his nature and partly the result of drink. For he was fond of drink and often when he sallied forth he was blind drunk.' For this particular incident, after the victory at Chaeronea, cf. also DS XVI.87, 1-3; Plut. *Dem*. XX. According to Justin's source (IX.5.1), however, Philip was modest in victory.

SELECTION OF RELEVANT INSCRIPTIONS

These are all taken from Volume II of Tod's *GHI*. The text is often defective owing to the condition of the stones on which the inscriptions were cut. The conjectural restorations accepted by Tod are here translated without any attempt to show where such reconstructions begin and end. Where restoration is impossible—particularly the case at the top and bottom of a stone—the lacuna in the text is here indicated by dots. These, it should be noted, do not show (as is the epigraphical convention) the number of missing letters in the text. Since Tod provides a commentary on each inscription, only some technical terms are explained here.

Tod 150   PHILIP CAPTURES AMPHIPOLIS, 357 BC

A decree of the people that: Philon and Stratokles together with their children shall go into perpetual exile from Amphipolis and from the territory of the Amphipolitans; and if they are seized anywhere (i.e., within Amphipolitan territory) they shall be treated as enemies and put to death, with no punishment resulting to their killers, and their property shall be confiscated with one-tenth of it to be dedicated to Apollo and the Strymon. The *prostatai*[1] shall inscribe their names on a stone *stele*. If anyone attempts to rescind the decree or harbours these men by any device or stratagem whatsoever his own property shall be confiscated and he himself shall go into perpetual exile from Amphipolis.

Tod 151   ALLIANCE BETWEEN ATHENS AND THRACIAN KINGS, 357 BC

... and concerning the cities which were inscribed on the stone *stelai* as paying tribute to Berisades or Amadokos or Kersebleptes[2] and which are already tributary to the Athenians: if these cities do not pay their tribute to the Athenians, Berisades, Amadokos and Kersebleptes shall exact the money so far as they are able; and if in any way these cities do not pay their tribute to Berisades or Amadokos or Kersebleptes, the

---

[1] *Prostates*: the title of an Amphipolitan magistrate.

[2] The inscription uses this spelling throughout; 'Kersobleptes' is the normal spelling in the literary sources.

Selection of Relevant Inscriptions

Athenians and those of their magistrates holding office at that particular time[3] shall exact the money so far as they are able. The Greek cities on the Chersonese which pay the traditional tribute to Berisades and Amadokos and Kersebleptes and the contribution to the Athenians shall be free and autonomous, being allies of the Athenians in accordance with the oaths they swore and of Berisades, Amadokos and Kersebleptes. If any of these cities revolts from the Athenians, Berisades and Amadokos and Kersebleptes shall assist in its recovery in accordance with any demands the Athenians might make; and if ...

Tod 153 ALLIANCE OF ATHENS AND EUBOEAN CITIES, 357/6 BC

... the prytany-secretary[4] shall see to the inscribing of this decree on the Acropolis; and the Treasurer shall provide the money for the stone *stele* from the sums spent on matters appertaining to decrees. Five men shall be elected to go and receive the oaths from the Karystians; and the regimental commanders,[5] the generals and the Council shall swear the oaths to them (i.e., to the Karystians). The Karystian People, the envoys of the Karystians and the Karystian Deputy[6] shall be commended publicly and shall be invited to dine the following day at the Prytaneum. Public commendation shall also be given to the general Menon and the envoys who have been sent to Karystos and they shall be invited to dine the following day at the Prytaneum. Moreover, the Treasurer of the People shall pay to them 20 drachmai as travelling expenses from the sums that are spent by the People on matters appertaining to decrees. The Treasurer of the People shall also pay 20 drachmai each to the envoys who have gone to Eretria and Chalkis and Histiaia; while to those who went as envoys to negotiate the alliance the Treasurer of the People shall pay 10 drachmai each. The following swore the oaths (i.e., on behalf of Athens):

The Council in office in the archonship of Agathokles
The Generals: Chabrias of the deme Aixone
Chares of the deme Angele

[3] Another possible translation of this phrase is 'those of their officers who are in command of the military force at that particular time'—referring to the military force stationed at the Chersonese.
[4] This official, whose office was instituted c. 367 BC, 'supervised the copying, registering and preserving of all State documents, and (at first) arranged for their publication when this was ordered; his name was normally put at the head of a published document as a guarantee of its accuracy'; A. W. Gomme, OCD, under 'Grammateis'. The Prytany-secretary is to be distinguished from the secretary of the council.
[5] I.e., the *taxiarchoi*; see IV.26 and note.
[6] I.e., the representative of the Karystian People that sat in the synod of Athens' Allies.

The Spectre of Philip

Iphikrates of the deme Rhamnous
Menon of the deme Potamos
Philochares of the deme Rhamnous
Exekestides of the deme Thorikos
Alkimachos of the deme Anagyros
Diokles of the deme Alopeke

Tod 154   ATHENS AIDS ERETRIA, 357/6 BC

A decree of the People; Hegesippos was the proposer of the motion that: in order that in the future none of the Athenian People nor anyone else, whether foreigner or citizen, may harm any of the allies by using any place in Attica as a base for operations, it should be decreed by the People that: concerning those who invaded the territory of the Eretrians the council shall draft a *probouleuma*[7] and submit it to the People at the first meeting of the assembly, in order that they (i.e., the invaders) may be punished according to the treaty. If in future anyone invades Eretria or any other of the cities that are in alliance with the Athenians or the allies of the Athenians he shall be condemned to death and his property shall be confiscated, one-tenth going to the Goddess;[8] and such property shall be recoverable from all the allied cities. If any city appropriates (any of this property), that city shall owe it to the League of the Allies. The decree shall be inscribed on a stone *stele* and set up on the Acropolis, in the Agora and at the harbour. The Treasurer of the People shall provide the money for the inscribing of the decree. Moreover, public commendation shall be given to those who went to the relief of Eretria . . .

Tod 155   ERYTHRAI HONOURS MAUSOLUS, 357-355 BC

A resolution of the council: the motion was proposed by the generals that: since Maussollus [sic], son of Hekatomnos, of Mylasa, has been a good man towards the city of the Erythraians, he shall be a benefactor, *proxenos*[9] and citizen of the city; and he shall have the right of entry into and departure from the city's harbour both in war-time and in peace, inviolably and without the need of a formal treaty; and he shall

---

[7] *Probouleuma*: a preliminary resolution drafted by the Council of 500 and submitted to the assembly for discussion and ratification (or amendment or rejection).

[8] I.e., Athena.

[9] *Proxenos*: briefly a citizen of community A officially protecting the interests of community B in his own community (A). The common translation 'consul' is misleading, since the modern consul is more usually (though not invariably) a citizen of community A resident in community B and there protecting the interests of his own community (A). Cf. OCD.

Selection of Relevant Inscriptions

have immunity from taxation and the right to a front seat in the theatre. These privileges shall be for himself and for his descendants. Moreover, a bronze statue of Maussollus shall be set up in the Agora and a stone statue of Artemisia in the temple of Athena; and a crown shall be presented to Maussollus, valued at 50 darics, and one to Artemisia, valued at 30 darics. The Public Auditors shall have these decisions inscribed on a *stele* and set up in the temple of Athena and shall supervise them (i.e., their execution).

Tod 156 ANDROS GARRISONED IN THE SOCIAL WAR, 356 BC

In the archonship of Agathokles; in the ninth prytany when Aigeis was the prytany-tribe and Diodotos, son of Diokles, of the deme Angele, was secretary; on the eighth day of the prytany; of the *Proedroi*[10] Diotimos, of the deme Oineia, put the motion to the vote: a decree of the Council and the People; Hegesandros was the proposer of the motion that: in order that Andros may be maintained in security for the Athenian People and in order that the garrison-troops on Andros may be paid from the contributions in accordance with the resolutions of the allies and in order that the garrison may not be disbanded, a general shall be chosen from those who have been elected and he who is chosen shall be in charge of Andros. Archedemos shall also exact the sums of money from the island communities which are owed to the soldiers on Andros and shall hand them over to the governor on Andros, in order that the soldiers may receive their pay . . .

Tod 157 ATHENIAN ALLIANCE WITH THRACIAN, PAEONIAN AND ILLYRIAN KINGS, 356 BC

Secretary Lysias, sons of Lys—, of the deme Pithos. Alliance of the Athenians with Ketriporis the Thracian and his brothers and with Lyppeios the Paeonian and with Grabos the Illyrian: in the archonship of Elpinos, in the first prytany when Hippothontis was the prytany-tribe; of the *Proedroi*[11] Mnesarchos . . . put the motion to the vote: a decree of the council and the People; Kallisthenes was the proposer of the motion that: with the good fortune of the Athenian People, the alliance shall be accepted on the conditions which Monounios, the brother of Ketriporis, says were agreed upon by his brother and by the representative sent by the Athenian People to Ketriporis and his brothers and to Lyppeios the Paeonian and to Grabos the Illyrian. The *Proedroi*, who happen to hold office by lot, shall introduce to the People

---

[10] For the Athenian *proedros* see Jones, *Ath.Dem.*, p. 107.
[11] See note 10.

at the first meeting of the Assembly Monounios, the brother of Ketriporis and Peisianax and the envoys which have come from Lyppeios and Grabos and . . . the emissary from Chares; and they (i.e., the *Proedroi*) shall communicate to the People the resolution of the Council that 'it seems good to the council to accept the alliance, since . . .' Public commendation shall be given to Ketriporis and his brothers because they are good men towards the Athenian People; and public commendation shall also be given to Monounios, the brother who has come from Ketriporis, because of his excellent character and good will, and he shall be invited to hospitality on the following day at the Prytaneum. Peisianax shall also be commended publicly and invited to dine on the following day at the Prytaneum; and the envoys who have come from the other kings shall be invited to hospitality on the following day at the Prytaneum. If this decree should require any further addition, the council shall be competent to make it.

The following were chosen as envoys:

> Lysikrates of the deme Oinoe
> Antimachos . . .
> Thrason of the deme Erchia

(The Oath) I swear by Zeus and Earth and Sun and Poseidon and Athena and Ares: I shall be a friend and ally of Ketriporis and the brothers of Ketriporis; and I shall prosecute, along with Ketriporis, the war against Philip without deceit, with all my strength and to the best of my ability; and I shall not initiate steps to settle the war against Philip without Ketriporis and his brothers; and I shall join with Ketriporis and his brothers in reducing the strongholds which Philip is occupying; and especially I shall join with Ketriporis and his brothers in capturing Krenides; and I shall hand over . . .

Tod 158   ALLIANCE BETWEEN PHILIP II AND THE CHALCIDIANS, 356 BC

I shall be an ally in accordance with the agreed terms. On the Chalcidian side the federal magistrates and the envoys shall swear the oath to Philip; Philip himself and any others whom the Chalcidians may demand shall swear the oath to the Chalcidians. They shall swear the oath without deceit or guile: 'by Zeus, Earth, Sun and Poseidon, if we keep the terms of the oath may much good accrue to us, but if we break the oath may we suffer much harm'. Both sides shall swear the oath while offering up sacrifices. These articles shall be inscribed on a stone *stele* and the Oracle given by the god[12] concerning the alliance shall be set up in a dedicatory form, by the Chalcidians in the

[12] 'The god': Apollo, at Delphi.

Selection of Relevant Inscriptions

temple of Artemis at Olynthus and by Philip in the temple of the Olympian Zeus at Dion; and a copy of both the *stelai* and the Oracle shall be placed at Delphi. It shall be possible to amend by common agreement, within a period of three months, any of these articles that Philip and the Chalcidians decide upon.

(Delphic Oracle:) The god pronounced to the Chalcidians and to Philip that 'it is good and desirable that they should become friends and allies in accordance with the terms agreed upon; that they should sacrifice to and obtain favourable sacrificial omens from Zeus the Fulfiller of Prayers and All Highest, Apollo the Protector, Artemis Orthosia[13] and Hermes; that they should pray that the alliance will be attended by good fortune; and that they should send to Apollo at Pytho[14] offerings of gratitude and should make public offerings of thanksgiving'.

Tod 166   OLYNTHIAN REFUGEES AT ATHENS, 348/7 BC

... concerning those requests which the Olynthians decided were right and proper to be made by themselves as suppliants among the Athenian People and their allies: since the Olynthians, after becoming allies of the Athenian People and of their allies, have been driven from their city as the result of Philip's siege-operations and since they are asking for immunity from the alien-tax[15] at Athens, the People shall decide forthwith by open vote concerning their case, whether or not to give the immunity from the alien-tax to those of the Olynthians who have been driven out of their city. If, after the open vote has been taken, the People decides to grant them the immunity, the secretary of the council shall have inscribed on a stone *stele* on the Acropolis their names and the statement that they are in exile after having been driven out of their city as a result of Philip's siege-operations. For the inscribing of the *stele* ...

---

[13] 'Artemis Orthosia': more commonly known as Artemis Orthia.
[14] 'Pytho': the old name for Delphi.
[15] *See* IV.36 with note.

THE ATTIC YEAR

AUTUMN	July (*Hekatombaion*)	/ E / t / e / s / i / a / n / W / i / n / d / s	Beginning of the Attic year Panathenaic Festival
	August (*Metageitnion*)		Pythian Festival (Delphi)
	September (*Boedromion*)		Eleusinian Mysteries
	October (*Pyanepsion*)		
WINTER	November (*Maimakterion*)		
	December (*Poseideon*)	*Note.* These equivalences of Julian and Attic months are only approximate and make no allowance for intercalation; cf. B. D. Meritt, *The Athenian Year*, pp. 3-5 *et passim*.	
	January (*Gamelion*)		
SPRING	February (*Anthesterion*)		
	March (*Elaphebolion*)		The Great Dionysia
	April (*Mounychion*)		
SUMMER	May (*Thargelion*)		
	June (*Skirophorion*)		Olympic Festival (Olympia)

CHRONOLOGICAL TABLE
Summer 352 BC to late autumn 346 BC

352	Summer	Philip captures Pherae and Pagasae (II.9, 14 and notes)
		He advances to Thermopylae but is anticipated by Athenian forces (IV.17 and notes)
		He sets out for Thrace (I.13 and notes)
	November	News received in Athens that he is besieging Heraion Teichos (III.4)
		Athens votes an expedition—which lapses (III.4-5 with note)
351	September	Athens votes another, smaller expedition (ibid.)
	September/October (?)	Philip falls ill (ibid.)
		The expedition is recalled or re-routed to the Hellespont (ibid.)
	October/November	Philip recovers and marches on Chalcidice (I.13 and notes)
350	January (?)	Delivery of *Philippic* I (p. 13)
349	August/September (?)	Beginning of Macedonian attacks on Chalcidice (Cawkwell, CQ 1962, 130)
		First Olynthian appeal to Athens (ibid., 129)
		Delivery of *Olynthiac* II
		Delivery of *Olynthiac* I (p. 37)
		Athenian/Olynthian alliance (Cawkwell, CQ 1962, 130)
		Delivery of *Olynthiac* III (ibid., 133-4)
	September/October (?)	First expedition to Olynthus, under Chares (ibid., 130)
348	February/March	Euboean expedition (ibid., 129)
		Second Olynthian appeal to Athens (ibid., 131)

348	March/April	Second expedition to Olynthus, under Charidemus (ibid.)
	April/May (?)	The attack on Olynthus itself begins (ibid., 132)
	June	Final appeal from Olynthus The third expedition is sent, under Chares (ibid., 130-1)
	June/July (?)	Philip informs Athens of his desire for peace (Aes. II.12-17, Cawkwell, *REG* 1960, 417) Philocrates proposes inviting Philip to send envoys to discuss peace (ibid.) He consequently faces a *graphe paranomon*, is defended by Demosthenes and is acquitted (ibid.)
	September/October	The fall of Olynthus (Cawkwell, *CQ* 1962, 130) Arrival of the third expedition (ibid., 130-1)
347	Early summer (?)	Phalaecus is deprived of his command of the Phocian army (Cawkwell, *REG* 1960, 427)
	Beginning of Attic year	Demosthenes becomes a member of the Council of 500 (Aes. III.162) Aristodemus brings news of Philip's willingness to negotiate an alliance (Aes. II.15-17)
346	Early January (?)	Eubulus' decree to send envoys inviting all Greeks to form alliance against Philip (Cawkwell, *REG* 1960, 418-25) Phocis asks Athens for aid (ibid.)
	Late January (?)	Phalaecus regains control of the Phocian army and rejects Athenian aid (ibid., 433)
	February	First embassy dispatched to Philip to invite his envoys to discuss peace (ibid., 432-3)
	February/March	After meeting the embassy, Philip attacks Cersobleptes, king of Thrace (Aes. II.81)

Chronological Table

346	April	
		18 and 19 *Elaphebolion*: Deliberations on peace in the Athenian assembly; Philocrates' proposal is passed (Cawkwell, *REG* 1960, 432-8)
		24 *Elaphebolion*: receipt of Chares' letter concerning Cersobleptes' surrender at Hieron Oros (Aes. II.90ff.)
		25 *Elaphebolion*: special assembly; Athens 'abandons' Cersobleptes (Aes. III.73-74)
	May	3 *Mounychion*: Second embassy leaves for Pella to receive Philip's oaths (Aes. II.91-92)
		c.26 *Mounychion* (?): Second embassy arrives in Pella, but Philip is still in Thrace (XIX.156)
	June	c.23 *Thargelion* (?): Philip returns, but does not take the oaths immediately (ibid., and 158)
	July	c.10 *Skirophorion*: Philip takes the oaths at Pherae (ibid., and 58)
		13 *Skirophorion*: Second embassy returns to Athens, by which time Philip is at Thermopylae (ibid.)
		16 *Skirophorion*: special assembly; Philocrates proposes confirmation of the peace and its extension to Philip's descendants. Also agreed that Athens will use force on the Phocians if they refuse to hand over Delphi to the Amphictyons (XIX.34-35, 48-50)
		c.21 *Skirophorion*: Third embassy leaves to report these decisions to Philip (XIX.121-124)
		23 *Skirophorion*: Phocis surrenders to Philip; the embassy, undecided on what action to take, turns for home (XIX.59-60)
		27 *Skirophorion*: Special assembly in Piraeus hears of the surrender; fourth embassy dispatched to

The Spectre of Philip

	Thermopylae to watch developments (Aes. II.94-96, 138-141)
	End of the Sacred War
	Demosthenes and Timarchus bring an action against Aeschines for misconduct on an embassy—the second in particular (Goodwin, pp. 302, 333)
346 August/September	Meeting of the Amphictyonic Council convened by Philip; the Phocians expelled and their votes given to Philip.
	The Pythian Games are held (ibid., pp. 302, 263-7)
	Envoys sent to Athens to demand her ratification of the Amphictyonic decisions (ibid., pp. 267-8)
	The speech *On the Peace* (? Libanius' Introduction to Speech V. 3 and note)

TABLE OF EXTANT GENUINE SPEECHES OF DEMOSTHENES TO 341

This table is not intended to be authoritative; controversy surrounds the genuineness and dating of many of the speeches and it is outside the purpose of this book to detail the various arguments. Our aim here is to indicate something of the progress of D.'s career through his speeches, and more particularly through those he himself elected to write and perhaps deliver, although in some cases they may not have reached the actual point of delivery. The speeches after 341 are omitted for two reasons: that many are difficult to date at all precisely, and that we are here concerned more with the rise than the peak of D.'s career. The speech *On the Crown* (XVIII), however, although it belongs late, must at least be mentioned, as it contains much of relevance to our period. It was delivered in August 330, but belongs to a prosecution initiated in 336 but delayed for 6 years. We have categorized the broad types of speech by the initials 'd' (*dikai*, 'purely private speeches'), 'g' (*graphai*, strictly, 'offences against the constitution', but here used a little more broadly, to cover appeals against earlier judgments and generally important cases) and 'p' ('public speeches', delivered in the Athenian Assembly).

Probable date	Speech no. in corpus	Title	Type of speech
363	XXVII	Against Aphobus I	d
	XXVIII	Against Aphobus II	d
	XXIX	Against Aphobus III	d
362	XXX	Against Onetor I	d
	XXXI	Against Onetor II	d
360–356	XLI	Against Spudias	d
	LV	Against Callicles	d
356	LIV	Against Conon	d
355	XX	Against Leptines	g
	XXII	Against Androtion	g
354	XIV	On the Navy Boards	p
353/2	XVI	For the Megalopolitans	p
	XXIV	Against Timocrates	g

The Spectre of Philip

Probable date	Speech no. in corpus	Title	Type of speech
352	XXIII	Against Aristocrates	g
351	XV	For the Liberty of the Rhodians	p
350	IV	Philippic I	p
	XXXVI	For Phormio	g
349	II	Olynthiac II	p
	I	Olynthiac I	p
	III	Olynthiac III	p
348 (?)	XXI	Against Meidias	d
	XLV	Against Stephanus I	g
346	XXXVII	Against Pantaenetus	g
	XXXVIII	Against Nausimachus	g
	V	On the Peace	p
344	VI	Philippic II	p
343	XIX	On the False Embassy	g
341	XXXIII	Against Apaturius	g
	XXXV	Against Lacritus	g
	VIII	On the Chersonese	p
	IX	Philippic III	p
	X	Philippic IV	p

SELECT BIBLIOGRAPHY

(Commonly cited works are referred to by the author's surname and are marked with an asterisk.)

1. Books

Accame, S., *La lega ateniese del secolo IV a.C.*, Rome 1941.
*Adcock, F. E., *The Greek and Macedonian Art of War*, Berkeley 1957.
*Alexander, J. A., *Potidaea, Its History and Remains*, Georgia 1963.
Amit, M., *Athens and the Sea. A Study in Athenian Sea-Power*, Collection Latomus, Bruxelles 1965.
*Arnott, P. D., *An Introduction to the Greek Theatre*, London 1959.
*Beloch, K. J., *Griechische Geschichte*, 2nd edn, Vol. III, Berlin and Leipzig 1922-3.
*Berve, H., *Das Alexanderreich auf prosopographischer Grundlage*, Vol. I, München 1926.
*Blass, F., *Die Attische Beredsamkeit*, Vol. III, Part 1 (Demosthenes), Leipzig 1893; reprinted 1962.
Buchanan, J. J., *Theorika*, New York 1962.
Cambridge Ancient History, Vol. VI, London 1927.
*Cloché, P., *Démosthènes et la fin de la démocratie athénienne*, reprinted Paris 1957.
———, *Un Fondateur d'Empire, Philippe II, Roi de Macédoine*, Saint-Etienne 1955.
———, *Thèbes de Béotie*, Namur 1955.
*Daremberg, Ch. V. and Saglio, E., *Dictionnaire des antiquités grecques et romaines d'après les textes et les monuments*, Paris 1881.
Dascalakis, A., *The Hellenism of the Ancient Macedonians*, Thessaloniki 1965.
Deubner, L., *Attische Feste*, reprinted Darmstadt 1966.
*Dindorf, G., *Demosthenes* (Scholia), Vol. VIII, Oxford 1851.
*Ehrenberg, V., *The Greek State*, Oxford 1960.
*Glotz, G. and Cohen, R., *Histoire Grecque*, Vol. III, Paris 1936.
*Gomme, A. W., *A Historical Commentary on Thucydides*, London 1956.
*Goodwin, W. W. (ed.), *Demosthenes: De Corona*, London 1901.

Select Bibliography

*Griffith, G. T., *Mercenaries of the Hellenistic World*, London 1935.
*Grote, G., *History of Greece*, Vol. XI, London 1869.
*Gude, M., *A History of Olynthus*, Baltimore 1933.
Hammond, N. G. L., *A History of Greece to 322 B.C.*, London 1959.
*Hicks, E. L. and Hill, G. F., *Greek Historical Inscriptions*, London 1901 [H&H].
*Jacoby, F., *Die Fragmente der griechischen Historiker*, reprinted Leiden 1954-63.
*Jaeger, W., *Demosthenes*, New York 1938; reprinted 1963.
*Jones, A. H. M., *Athenian Democracy*, Oxford 1957.
*Kennedy, G., *The Art of Persuasion in Greece*, London 1963.
*Kromayer, J. and Veith, G., *Heerwesen und Kriegführung der Griechen und Römer*, München 1928.
*Marshall, F. H., *The Second Athenian Confederacy*, London 1905.
Meritt, B. D., *The Athenian Year*, Berkeley 1961.
Momigliano, A. D., *Filippo il Macedone, saggio sulla storia greca del IV secolo a.C.*, Florence 1934.
*Murray, G., *Greek Studies*, London 1946.
*Olmstead, A. T., *History of the Persian Empire*, Chicago 1948.
*Parke, H. W., *Greek mercenary soldiers from the earliest times to the battle of Ipsus*, London 1933.
*Pickard-Cambridge, A. W., *Demosthenes*, New York 1914.
Robertson, D. S., *A Handbook of Greek and Roman Architecture*, 2nd edn, London 1959.
*Ryder, T. T. B., *Koine Eirene*, London 1965.
Schaefer, A., *Demosthenes und seine Zeit*, 3 vols, reprinted Leipzig 1966.
*Sordi, M., *La lega tessala*, Rome 1958.
*Tarn, W. W., *Alexander the Great*, 2 vols, London 1948.
Tod, M. N., *A Selection of Greek Historical Inscriptions*, 2 vols, London 1948
I refer to Vol. II unless otherwise noted.
*Westlake, H. D., *Thessaly in the Fourth Century B.C.*, London 1935.
*Wüst, F., *Philipp II von Makedonien und Griechenland in den Jahren von 346 bis 338*, München 1938.

2. Articles

Adam, A. M., 'Philip alias Hitler', *G&R* X (1940/1), 105-113.
Andriotes, N. P., 'History of the Name Macedonia', *Balkan Studies* I (1960), 143-148.
Aymard, A., 'Basileus Makedonon', *RIDA* IV (1950), 61-97.
Bradeen, D., 'The Popularity of the Athenian Empire', *Historia* IX (1960), 257-269.

Select Bibliography

Cawkwell, G. L., 'Aeschines and the Peace of Philocrates', *REG* LXXIII (1960), 416-438.

———, 'Aeschines and the Ruin of Phocis', *REG* LXXV (1962), 453-459.

———, 'The Defence of Olynthus', *CQ* n.s. XII (1962), 122-140.

———, 'Demosthenes' Policy after the Peace of Philocrates', Part I, *CQ* n.s. XIII (1963), 120-138.

———, 'Eubulus', *JHS* LXXXIII (1963), 47-67.

———, 'Notes on the Social War', *C&M* XXIII (1962), 34-49.

Davison, J. A., 'Notes on the Panathenaea', *JHS* LXXVIII (1958), 23-42.

Ehrhardt, C., 'Two Notes on Philip's Interventions in Thessaly', *CQ* n.s. XVII (1967), 296-301.

Ellis, J. R., 'The Date of Demosthenes' First Philippic', *REG* LXXIX (1966), 636-639.

———, 'The Order of the Olynthiacs', *Historia* XVI (1967), 108-112.

Erbse, H., 'Zu den olynthischen Reden des Demosthenes', *RhM* n.s. XCIX (1956), 364-380.

Hammond, N. G. L., 'Diodorus' Narrative of the Sacred War', *JHS* LVII (1937), 44-68.

———, 'The Sources of Diodorus Siculus XVI (I)', *CQ* XXI (1937), 78-91.

———, 'The Sources of Diodorus Siculus XVI (II)', *CQ* XXII (1938), 135-151.

Harrison, A. R. W., 'Law-making at Athens at the end of the 5th C.', *JHS* LXXV (1955), 26-35.

Larsen, J. A. O., 'The Acharnians and the Pay of Taxiarchs', *CPh* XLI (1946), 91-98.

MacMullen R., 'Foreign Policy for the Polis', *G&R* X (1963), 118-122.

Milns, R. D., 'Philip II and the Hypaspists', *Historia* XVI (1967), 509-512.

———, 'Demosthenes III.35', *Eranos* LXVII (1969), 208-209.

Musurillo, H., 'A Critical Note on Demosthenes' First Philippic', *CQ* n.s. VII (1957), 86-88.

Parke, H. W., 'Athens and Euboea, 349/8 BC', *JHS* XLIX (1929), 246-252.

Pearson, L., 'The Development of Demosthenes as a Political Orator', *Phoenix* XVIII (1964), 95-109.

Perlman, S., 'The Politicians of the Athenian Democracy of the 4th C. BC', *Athenaeum* XLI (1963), 327-355.

———, 'Isocrates "Philippus"—a Reinterpretation', *Historia* VI (1957), 306-317.

Select Bibliography

Robbins, F. E., 'The Cost to Athens of her Second Empire', *CPh* XIII (1918), 361-388.

Roebuck, C., 'The Settlement of Philip II with the Greek States in 338 BC', *CPh* XLIII (1948), 73-92.

Ste Croix, G. E. M. de, 'The Character of the Athenian Empire', *Historia* III (1954/5), 1-41.

——, 'The Alleged Secret Pact between Athens and Philip II', *CQ* n.s. XIII (1963), 110-119.

Sealey, R., 'Athens after the Social War', *JHS* LXXV (1955), 74-81.

——, 'Dionysius of Halicarnassus and some Demosthenic Dates', *REG* LXVIII (1955), 77-120.

——, 'Proxenus and the Peace of Philocrates', *WS* LXVIII (1955), 145-152.

Treves, P., 'The Meaning of *consenesco* and King Arybbas of Epirus', *AJPh* LXIII (1942), 129-143.

Walbank, F. W., 'The Problem of Greek Nationality', *Phoenix* V (1951), 41-60.

West, A. B., 'The Early Diplomacy of Philip II of Macedon, Illustrated by his Coins', *NumChron* 1923, 169-210.

3. SOME SELECTED REVIEWS

The object of this selection is to enable the reader to see the opinions and criticisms of leading scholars on some of the more important books in this Bibliography. The reviews have been confined mainly to readily accessible periodicals in English. Only the first page number of each review is given.

Adcock, F. E., *CR* n.s. IX (1959), 268; *AJPh* LXXIX (1958), 448; *Phoenix* XIII (1959), 88.

Berve, H., *JHS* XLVI (1926), 283; *CR* XLI (1927), 39.

Cambridge Ancient History VI, *JHS* XLVII (1927), 285; *CR* XLII (1928), 183; *CJ* XXV (1929), 242.

Cloché, P., *Un Fondateur d'Empire, Philippe II, Roi de Macédoine*, *CR* n.s. VIII (1958), 156.

——, *Démosthènes et la fin de la démocratie athénienne*, *CR* LI (1937), 177.

Griffith, G. T., *CR* XLIX (1935), 136; *CJ* XXXI (1936), 455; *REA* XLVII (1935), 489; *REG* XLIX (1936), 93.

Jaeger, W., *JHS* LVIII (1938), 263.

Jones, A. H. M., *CR* n.s. IX (1959), 60; *JHS* LXXIX (1959) 182, *CPh* LIV (1959), 139.

Marshall, F. H., *JHS* XXVII (1907), 308.

Momigliano, A. D., *JHS* LV (1935), 98; *CR* L (1936), 32.

Parke, H. W., *CR* XLVII (1933), 226; *REG* XLVIII (1935), 153.

Select Bibliography

Pickard-Cambridge, A. W., *JHS* XXXIV (1914), 332.
Ryder, T. T. B., *Gnomon* XXXVIII (1966), 256.
Sordi, M., *JHS* LXXX (1960), 223; *AJA* LXIV (1960), 104; *CPh* LV (1960), 229; *CR* X (1960), 55.
Westlake, H. D., *JHS* LV (1935), 254; *REG* XLIX (1936), 611; *CR* XLIX (1935), 186.
Wüst, F., *CR* LII (1938), 232; *REG* LII (1939), 209.

INDEX

Abdera, 17
Aeschines, 2, 42, 79, 82, 85
Agathocles, 98
Agyrrhios, 94
Alexander II, 50, 97
Alexander III (the Great), 1, 4, 49, 50
Alexander of Epirus, 59
Alkimachos, 104
Amadokos, 102f.
Amphictyonic League, 79, 81f., 86ff.
Amphipolis, 17, 19, 27, 31, 35, 45f., 53, 55, 56ff., 81, 85f., 89, 97f., 102
Amyntas III, 10, 39
Amyntas (nephew of Philip), 10
Andros, 105
Anthemus, 39, 46
Antimachos, 106
Antipater, 79, 100
Antiphon, 97
Apollodorus, 36, 43, 92
Arcadia, 87
Archedemos, 105
Argaios, 10
'Argas', 8
Argos, 86f.
Aristides, 71f.
Aristonicus, 101
Artabazus, 23
Artemisia, 68, 105
Arybbas, 59
Athenians (attitudes and policies), 5, 10, 15, 18, 19, 35, 36f., 44, 49, 52, 55ff., 65, 69, 71ff., 77ff., 81f., 83f., 91ff., 101, 102f., 104, 105f.
Athenian Second League, 6, 11, 25, 35, 65, 86, 103, 104, 105 See also Social War
Attica, 68, 82

'Batalos', 8
Berisades, 102f.

Boedromia, 74
Boeotia, 10, 81, 86
Bottiaia, 95
Byzantium, 10, 11, 18, 23, 31, 33, 49, 89

Callias, 51
Callistratus, 8
Cardia, 89
Caria, 89
Cersobleptes, 78f., 102f.
Chabrias, 23, 103
Chaeronea, Battle of, 4, 24, 101
Chalcidians, 19, 24, 27, 34ff., 39, 44, 46, 49, 56, 67, 95, 98f., 106 See also Olynthus
Chalcis, 39, 103
Chares, 23, 31, 36, 52, 95, 103, 106
Charidemus, 31, 36, 66, 77, 95, 97
Chersonese, 12, 21, 30, 55, 79, 103
Chios, 10, 89
choregos, 28
cleruchies, 46
Corinth, 5, 23, 39, 71, 96
Corinth, League of, 5f.
Corinthian War, 4, 23, 39
corn-route, 12, 27, 28, 89
Cos, 89

Delos, 28
Delphi, 5, 10, 79, 88ff., 95f., 106f.
Demosthenes (career and policies), 2ff., 7, 8ff., 11ff., 15, 19ff., 36, 42, 51, 53, 60f., 78ff., 84ff., 91ff.
Diokles, 104
Dionysia, 28
Diopeithes, 79
Doron, 101

Egypt, 68
eisphora 18, 26, 48, 52ff., 61, 66
Eleusinian Mysteries, 24, 66

120

Index

Epaminondas, 73
Ephialtes, 95
Epirus, 49, 59
Eretria, 35f., 87, 103, 104
Erythrai, 104
Etesian winds, 15, 26, 37, 77
Euboea, 21, 29f., 35f., 39, 57, 63, 75, 77, 84f., 92
Eubulus, 2, 11, 12, 16, 30, 69, 73, 78, 84, 91ff., 96, 98
Eurydice, 10
euthyna, 32, 43, 64
Exekestides, 104

Geraistos, 28
Gonnos, 98
Grabos, 105f.
graphe paranomon, 36, 43, 69, 74, 92
gymnasiarchos, 28

Haliartus, 21
Halonnesos, 27
Hellespont, 36f., 49, 67, 79
Heraion Teichos, 11, 18, 21, 30, 59, 66
hetairoi, 49f., 97, 99ff.
Hierax, 57
Hieroclides, 95f.
hierophantes, 95
hieropoios, 24
hipparchos, 24
Histiaia, 103
hypaspists, 25

Idreus, 89
Illyria, 32, 49, 59, 62, 105f.
Imbros, 28
Iphicrates, 23, 104
Isthmia, 96

Karystos, 103
Kersobleptes *see* Cersobleptes
Ketriporis, 105f.
King's Peace, 27
Koroneia, 81, 88

Lacratides, 95f.
Lemnos, 26f., 28
Leuctra, Battle of, 10, 17
liturgies, 28, 85
logistai, 64
Lyppeios, 105f.
Lysikrates, 106

Macedonia, 3, 6, 10, 17, 19, 21, 27, 33, 35, 39f., 42, 45, 47ff., 60, 67, 70, 73, 81f., 84f., 106
Magnesia, 38, 46ff., 58, 62
Mantinea, Battle of, 73
Marathon, 28
Maronea, 17
Mausolus, 11, 89, 104f.
Megalopolis, 87
Megara, 71, 95f.
Meidias, 84
Menelaus the Pelagonian, 24, 48
Menon, 103f.
mercenaries, 6, 15, 20ff., 29, 32, 37, 49, 53, 69, 76
Messene, 87
Methone, 17, 26, 34, 57f.
metoikoi, 29, 107
Miletus, 89
Military fund *see stratiotikon*
Miltiades, 72
Molossus, 77
Monounios, 105f.
Mylasa, 104

Neoptolemus, 84f.
Nicias, 71
nomothetai, 68

Olympias, 59
Olynthus, 2, 12ff., 21, 26, 34ff., 39ff., 44ff., 55ff., 67ff., 77f., 95, 98f., 107
Onomarchus, 34
Orchomenos, 81, 88
Oropus, 8, 85, 87, 89

Paeonia, 49, 59, 62, 105f.
Pagasae, 17, 26, 38, 48, 57f., 62
Pallene, 95
Panathenaia, 28
Pangaeus, Mount, 3, 27
Parmenion, 79
Peisianax, 106
Pella, 4, 79, 84
Peloponnesian War, 4, 6, 39
penestai, 98
Peparethos, 27
Perdiccas II, 39, 72
Perdiccas III, 10, 48
Pericles, 5, 40, 71
Perinthus, 11, 18, 33, 49
Perrhaebaea, 98
Persia, 4, 6, 23, 30, 32, 68, 89, 95

Index

pezetairoi, 50, 97
Phalaecus, 78f.
Pherae, 17, 34, 49, 58, 79
Philip II, 1ff., 10, 17, 18, 19, 30, 39ff., 45, 47, 49ff., 56, 58f., 62, 66, 70, 73, 77ff., 85ff., 95, 98, 99ff., 106, 107
Philochares, 104
Philocrates and Peace of P., 18, 78f., 82, 89, 96
Philon, 102
Phocion, 35, 77
Phocis, 5, 10, 34, 47, 58, 63, 68, 78ff., 81, 85
phoros, 86
phylarchos, 24
Plataea, 85
Plutarchus of Eretria, 35f., 84
Pnyx, 45
Polystratus, 23
Potidaea, 17, 26, 39, 46, 48, 57f., 97
Propontis, 11
proxenos, 104
Proxenus, 78
Pydna, 17, 46, 56ff., 97f.
Pytheas, 9
Pythia, 80, 88

Rhodes, 10, 89

Sacred War, 10, 47, 63, 73, 78ff., 88
Sciathos, 26f.
Skopelos, 27

Social War, 10, 11, 17, 23, 30, 35, 46, 57, 73, 89, 92
Sparta, 3, 10, 17, 23, 32, 39, 52, 73, 87
strategos, 24, 32, 53
stratiotikon, 40f., 43, 61, 69f., 75f., 91ff., 94
Stratocles, 57, 102
Strymon, 102
symmoriai, 53, 94

Tamynae, 77
taxiarchos, 24
Tempe, 98
Thasos, 26f.
Thebes, 5, 10, 32, 63, 68, 73, 81, 85ff., 95
Themison of Eretria, 87
theorikon, 36, 38, 40f., 43, 60, 68ff., 74ff., 91ff., 94, 98
Thermopylae, 11, 14, 21, 30, 52, 66, 73, 78f., 81f., 85
Thespiae, 85
Thessaly, 17, 19, 27, 35, 38, 46ff., 49, 58, 61, 63, 79, 81, 86, 98, 99
Thrace, 11f., 14, 21, 30, 39, 49, 59, 62, 66ff., 78f., 105f.
Thrason, 106
Timotheus, 24, 31, 48
traitors, 4, 22
trierarchos, 20, 29, 54

xenoi, 49f.

OHIO UNIVERSITY LIBRARY